Praise for *From Sylhet*

CW01053404

This important and inspiring book recovers the radical history of the Bengali squatters' movement active in Tower Hamlets in the 1970s. Through sparkling vignettes of the individuals involved, Begum provides deep insights into the forms of solidarity that sustained the movement and the political differences that also characterised it. It's a powerful contribution to working-class and multicultural histories of Britain.

Gurminder K. Bhambra, Professor of Postcolonial and Decolonial Studies (Global Studies), University of Sussex

Shabna Begum has written a brilliantly nuanced and long overdue study of the Bengali squatters' movement in 1970s London. Through foregrounding varied and vivid voices of Bengali women and men of different generations and experiences, she demonstrates how their claims to dilapidated houses, as they faced down violent physical and institutional racism, were integral to a shared struggle to establish their rights as equal citizens.

From Sylhet to Spitalfields captures how the battles for housing of British Bengalis and their allies were, in different ways, framed by anticolonial imaginations and the Bangladesh Liberation War.

Georgie Wemyss, Co-Director, Centre for Research on Migration, Refugees and Belonging (CMRB) at the University of East London

For too long, Britain's postcolonial migrants have been neglected by histories of squatting and housing campaigns. *From Sylhet to Spitalfields* brings to life the community-based anti-racists that struggled for housing in East London, and a home in Britain. Begum's moving accounts and sharp analysis are crucial for understanding how the right to housing is bound up with freedom from racism.

Adam Elliott-Cooper, author of *Black Resistance to British Policing* (Manchester University Press, 2021).

Begum covers a fascinating yet neglected aspect of British South Asian history. The book details, with great vigour, the necessary political activism Bangladeshi communities engaged in in the 1960s and 1970s to forge a better life for themselves and those who came after them. An engaging read, reflecting on and critically evaluating the historic political activism that has shaped the lives of British Bangladeshis in the present.

Taj Ali, Industrial Correspondent at *Tribune* magazine

From Sylhet to Spitalfields

Bengali Squatters in 1970s East London

Shabna Begum

Lawrence Wishart
London 2023

Lawrence and Wishart Limited
Central Books Building
Freshwater Road
Chadwell Heath
RM8 1RX

Typesetting: e-type
Cover design: Isabel Lecaros
Printing: Imprint Digital

First published 2023
© Shabna Begum 2023

British Library Cataloguing in Publication Data.
A catalogue record for this book is available from the British Library

ISBN 9781913546748
E-format ISBN: 9781913546755

For Anisah and Ihsan

Contents

INTRODUCTION

Number 12 Deal Street

A personal family photograph from 1976.

This photograph shows Abdul Masabbir and Guljahan Begum, their three-year-old daughter Rasna and me as a seven-month-old baby. The photograph was taken in late 1976, just after my migrant parents left their 'accidental squat' a few minutes' walk from Brick Lane. Unlike other Bengali migrants, they had not deliberately squatted.[1] They had paid a significant sum of money to obtain a rent book from a man who had posed as a landlord of a small, cottage-style house at 12 Deal Street, E1. I was born within weeks of them having settled into what they had thought was their newly rented property. They were devastated when they found out that the council in fact owned the house and there was a closing order on it, meaning it was due to be demolished and rebuilt. Council officials came and served them notice to leave, but my parents had paid a small fortune for the 'rent book' and they had nowhere else to go, so they stayed on as accidental squatters, joining a growing number of Bengali families who were unable to meet their housing need any other way.

Shortly after, my parents left Tower Hamlets, just before the wider squatter movement exploded on their former doorstep in the hot summer of 1976. Despite their brief and unsuccessful encounter with squatting, they would occasionally speak of this time of great hardship and challenge, and it is from the seeds of those conversations that, nearly half a century later, this book has emerged.

This book takes my parents' experience as a starting point but engages with a much wider migrant squatter movement that has, until recently, received little attention. Up until the 1970s the Bengali migrant community had been mainly single Bengali men, some commuting for decades between Sylhet and London, working in low-paid jobs and living in shared accommodation, sometimes in beds that were rotated in double and triple shifts. However, by the mid 1970s, and with increased racialised restrictions on Commonwealth migration, these men started to bring their families over to the UK, worried that, if not, they might be permanently separated by the legislative barriers that were being erected.[2]

With newly arrived families, the hostel-style accommodation for that had for decades served single men was no longer an appropriate model of housing. However, Tower Hamlets' waiting list rules meant they did not qualify for council properties, and many families found themselves trapped in overcrowded flats as they tried to navigate a system that systematically discriminated against them. Those families that were fortunate enough to secure a tenancy were often given the worst accommodation. These tenancies were usually in the flats and houses from which existing white tenants had been decanted and rehoused, and frequently in parts of the borough where Bengali families were isolated from their community and subject to racist attacks. With pockets of highly visible white squatter communities around them, individual Bengali families began to take direct action and help themselves to the abundance of empty, boarded-up properties in and around Spitalfields.

By 1976 the shared experience of confronting an institutionally racist housing system and the ferocious rise of National Front violence prompted the shift from individualised to community responses. With the support of *Race Today* activists, Bengali squatters organised into a loosely knit squatters' organisation. They challenged Tower Hamlets Council and the Greater London Council (GLC) to provide fairer housing options for the community. The 1949 Ordnance Survey Map shows some of the areas in which Bengali squatters occupied properties including Deal Street, where my parents stayed.

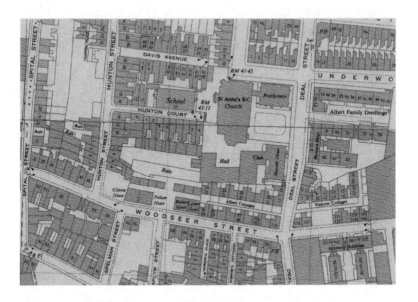

OS map published 1949. Reproduced with the permission of National Library of Scotland. The map shows Deal Street in the top right, where my parents first stayed. Further down you can see Schwartz Building, which later became Pelham Buildings, a key Bengali squatter site.

Initially, squatting in the Bengali community began with small numbers of families desperate to secure accommodation for themselves, often assisted by white squatters. Over the decade those numbers swelled to hundreds of families, and by spring 1976 the Bengali Housing Action Group, or BHAG, which means 'share' or 'tiger' in Bengali, was created. This largely informal organisation worked to secure squats for Bengali families in need, protect them against eviction and defend them against racist attacks. Some of the younger male squatters organised wider vigilante patrols against racist attacks, which grew into the more well-known anti-racist mobilisations of the late 1970s following the racist murder of Altab Ali in 1978.

While the men may have been active on the streets, it was Bengali women who were guardians of their squatted homes, confronting hostile estate managers and neighbours as they resisted eviction and harassment. By late 1977 the GLC, which was overwhelmed by the widespread nature of squatting, announced an amnesty and invited all squatters to register and secure a formal tenancy. BHAG managed to negotiate tenancies within a defined and agreeable area, and Bengali families were either given tenancies in the places they had occupied or in new accommodation. This was by no means a happy ending as Bengali migrant families continued to experience racialised discrimination in Tower Hamlets housing allocation over the next few decades, but the Bengali squatters had asserted and won a right to social housing that had previously been denied to them.

The radical history of this generation is only now being brought to light. My sense of urgency in conducting this research came as many in the generation of Bengali migrants who had been involved in the squatting movement are now elderly – some have already passed away. Few have ever been asked for their stories; many had internalised the years of indifference to this history and were therefore surprised at this late enquiry. It is also interesting to observe younger Bengali activists involved in contemporary local campaigns like the Save Brick Lane campaign – an initiative which is fighting the displacement of Bengali people from E1 as a result of gentrification – taking inspiration from this history.

The impact of commercial and residential gentrification on working-class and racialised communities is evident all over London and in other cities in the UK but is hyper-intensified in Tower Hamlets, which borders the financial district and Canary Wharf. New housing developments are being built with dubious notions of 'affordability', displacing thousands of social housing tenants. In a recent refurbishment of Balfron Tower, a brutalist tower block in Poplar, social housing tenants were 'decanted' with vague commitments that they might be able to return to their homes, only for that refurbishment to result in a private, leaseholder-only block, where one-bedroom flats are being sold for £375,000, and four-bedroom flats at £800,000.

The inequities of the housing system have been further exposed during the Covid-19 pandemic, as many struggled to pay their rent and feared eviction, while others invested in spacious second homes. There is also the ongoing inquiry into the devastating fire at Grenfell Tower that killed seventy-two people in a block owned by the Royal Borough of Kensington and Chelsea – one of the wealthiest councils in the UK – which spent money cosmetically enhancing the exterior with inferior quality cladding but failed to install basic sprinkler systems and fire alarms. The fact that it was disproportionately people of colour who died in the fire, and indeed communities of colour that continue to experience higher levels of housing stress, is not news.[3] It is telling, but promising, that Justice4Grenfell campaigners have been making connections with housing campaign groups in Tower Hamlets such as Justice4THCH – who have been campaigning about the years of neglect and disrepair of their buildings and homes – exploring how, together, these groups might build collective resistance to social housing injustice.

HERE AND THERE

While it is possible to construct some partial accounts of the history of Bengali squatters from reports in popular and academic literature, none of the existing records register the events from the perspective of Bengali migrants themselves. This illustrates the way that the community's role and significance has been undermined in the history of squatting to date, a pattern which this book seeks to

disrupt using first-hand oral history interviews with former squatters. In doing so, it has become not just a history of a particular part
of the squatting movement in Britain but of the Bengali community's settlement in the UK in a wider sense.

Talking to former squatters, it quickly became clear that Bengali
migrants in this period were not a homogenous group. Generation
and gender differences were important factors in how people
saw themselves and their experience; for example, older migrants
carried different attachments to 'back home' than younger people,
and gender had an important impact on both their initial migration journeys and their experiences upon arrival. My efforts here
seek to reflect that diversity and to represent the squatters with
their different, sometimes inconsistent and divergent perspectives.
Some were activist squatters who celebrated and cherished their
squatting memories, others were more ambivalent, perhaps even
ashamed of the housing deprivation that pushed them into squatting. Whichever way they positioned themselves in relation to these
events, this book tries to offer the fullness of that untidy mosaic,
rather than harry them into a tidy narrative.

A postcolonial lens helps to understand how the Bengali community arrived in East London in the first place, and how colonially
rooted, racialised tropes underpinned the discrimination they
confronted. Institutional discrimination against Bengali migrants
in housing was compounded by street racism, in the form of brutal
violence inflicted by the National Front and the routine hostility of
neighbours. This can be seen as a form of 'un-homing': a process
designed to deny the Bengali migrant community the right or ability
to make a home. These interactive racisms relied on a depiction of
the Bengali community as 'alien' and outside of the 'community of
belonging' of the 'real' East End, which was imagined as essentially
and rightfully white.[4] This state and street violence depended on
long-standing racialised tropes that were actively cultivated during
Empire about Bengali cultural inferiority and effeminacy.

Drawing on transnational perspectives also broadens the focus
by remembering that Bengali migrants retained multiple, enduring
and evolving relationships to both their place of 'origin' and where
they settled, and that these connections were an important matrix
for how they managed racist hostility and their homemaking

ambitions.[5] In the book, I trace how *here* – Spitalfields – and *there* – Sylhet – are connected and interactive spaces, made and remade in the actions and affections of migrants. Bengali migrants were not just actors navigating a colonially scripted migration story – they carried and sustained inheritances from *there* which shaped their understanding of home and resistance *here*. For example, older migrants, often with considerable financial responsibilities, were generally committed to maintaining strong relationships with 'back home'; being in London was considered an extended working arrangement, rendered tolerable by trips back to Bangladesh. In this transnational home imaginary, migrants remitted their earnings to family and built *Londoni* homes to which they planned to return.[6] Some former squatters I interviewed explained how this deferral of gratification allowed them to tolerate the hard and hostile working conditions they encountered in London.

For the younger generation there were fewer family and remittance ties and generally a little more freedom in how they navigated life in the UK. Many were young enough to have had some schooling in Britain and therefore developed more expectations for the right to stay and make home. The differences in these transnational relationships are critical to understanding those who saw squatting as simply another way to survive and claim space – even if temporarily, while planning a return home – and those who saw squatting as part of a bold claim to social resources from which they were being illegitimately excluded.

Another important theme in the book relates to ideas about 'home' and 'belonging'. These may be everyday terms, but they can also be deeply evocative, diversely understood and even discordant. This book explores squatting as a claim to making home in a racially hostile and exclusionary space. Using scholarship on migrant home and home-making, and in particular what are described as 'critical geographies' of home, I think about home as simultaneously *material* and *imaginative* – that is, both a physical place and an affective idea – so that it may be a specific dwelling or perhaps a fond memory of a childhood house, or a combination of both. Home may also reflect relationships of power and can produce and articulate identities, in particular ideas around belonging. Finally, this critical perspective understands home as *multi-scalar,* which speaks to the different layers or extensions of home, such as the way that we may feel 'at home' in places other than our immediate house: in a neighbourhood, a city or even a 'nation'.[7]

One of the benefits of using oral history was being able to span some forty-five years of experience, making it possible to trace how these attachments to 'here' and 'there' have shifted over the course of a lifetime. I reflect how decisions about where 'home' was in the 1970s were directed by the priorities of migrant men and their extended families, but often, over the course of their lifetime, those decisions became dominated by the maternal and grandmaternal authority of older Bengali women, who no longer conceded that authority to their husbands and families. Homemaking ambitions that once straddled Sylhet and Spitalfields in uncertain ways shifted as these women began acknowledging that their home attachments were no longer tied to Sylhet but rather London – and often, most importantly, with their multi-generational families there.

SITUATING SQUATTING

This book also draws on and challenges some of the existing scholarship around geographies of squatting. To date, academic work on squatting in the Global North has tended to focus on 'autonomous' squatter movements, which are deemed 'politically significant' because they challenge how property is distributed and are overtly counter-cultural.[8] This tendency seems to come from a distinction between 'deprivation' squatting, or squatting that emerges out of necessity, and 'political squatting', which is undertaken by people who are explicitly acting in opposition to the existing housing system.[9] Though this distinction can in many ways be helpful, it has tended to distract from the deeply political – and in this case racialised – reasons for the housing deprivation experienced by Bengali squatters, and undermines the inherently political nature of entering and occupying an empty property in response to that deprivation.

For Bengali migrants in the racially hostile East London of the 1970s, squatting was a claim to social housing and to the right to be able to feel safe in the city. Bengali squatters challenged the narrative about who belonged and who had earned their place in the East End and, through their refusal to be dispersed and dispossessed, refused to accept whiteness as a proxy for belonging. To deny the political nature of this squatting is a disservice to these events. There was also a more intimate claim for home that underpinned these events. For Bengali migrants, home extended to zones outside of the physical space, which in Sylhet is known as *para*, or neighbourhood, so the way that squatting developed into wider vigilante movements to secure the streets in Spitalfields was also about that *here/there* imagination, remaking something of that extended sense of home they had previously enjoyed.

TELLING STORIES

This research was arrived at through an unexpected personal journey. What my parents related to me about their early migration journey described an important period of East London social history, yet my initial research bore little fruit. Looking through the archives, it was the frugality of records and information, the partial references and oblique glimpses, which became the incentive for further research. Through my early efforts, I discovered a few intimations about the existence of Bengali squatters in a collection about 1970s squatter history titled *Squatting: The Real Story*, by Nick Wates and Christian Wolmer. However, in this 230-page book, Bengali squatters are mentioned in just one short section.[10] Then, of course, there are the acclaimed photographs by David Hoffman. Hoffman himself was a squatter in 1970s East London and his album about squatting has been exhibited both in London and internationally. Photographs with unnamed Bengali children seen playing in the streets outside Fieldgate Mansions hint at the presence of Bengali squatters, yet the stories of the Bengali figures captured in those images were never collected. Hoffman generously and enthusiastically gave me permission to use his photos. He was eager to hear about the progress of my research, but he was also frank that his interaction with the Bengali community of squatters was limited, and he had no details about the Bengali people in his photographs. Bengali migrant squatters are therefore only *peripher-*

ally visible; they appear as an exotic Other that add curiosity and intrigue to an extraordinary collection of images, but through the images alone we are unable to know anything else about them.

Fieldgate Mansions © David Hoffman.

The muted presence of Bengali squatters in existing accounts raised many questions about whose stories are told and listened to. Why were accounts which were otherwise so precise in their detail so inattentive to what must also have been there in plain sight?

And more fundamentally, how does the erasure of certain *historical* geographies actively contribute to contemporary geographies of exclusion and marginalisation? By focusing on a particular profile of white 'counter-cultural' squatters, the archives as they currently exist present a distorted view of the housing struggles of this period and erase Bengali migrants' role in resisting racialised exclusion in 1970s London.

For these reasons, this book takes a critical approach to the modest archival records and how they have represented the Bengali squatter. Drawing on feminist methodologies, I am attentive to the fact that the archives, when capable of telling anything of this story, used an externalised lens that gave little space for Bengali migrants to *speak for themselves*. This book is an attempt to counter that by sharing the events and experiences of 1970s Bengali squatting in a way that remains close to the voices of the people that lived them.

At the heart of this book is a collection of Bengali migrant squatter experiences generated by hundreds of hours of oral history interviews that I conducted in both Bengali and English. By spending time in elderly people's community centres and reaching out through social media networks, I was able to interview just over forty Bengali squatters and squatter activists, including my parents. Most of the accounts offered here use the real name of the person because as oral histories they form an archive for this period. However, there are some people who did not want to be publicly identifiable and where that was the case, I have indicated that I am using a pseudonym. Of course, there are limitations to oral history research, namely that they are individualised, bilateral conversations about complex, community-based events. They are also problematic because as a researcher, I took oral accounts and flattened them out into text to represent them here. The choice of words included is filtered through my editorial lens, particularly where I have translated interviews from Bengali into English, which involves considerable subjective interpretation. It is also important to note that each participant gave me considerable time to collect their story. For this work, I offer only a glimpse of their overall accounts,

Nevertheless, this book also represents the first time that some of these participants have spoken about their experiences to a researcher who many of them saw as *nijor manush*, or 'one of our own'. It challenges their erasure in previous accounts and begins to set out why this movement was not only important to the migrant homemaking ambitions of the Bengali community in the 1970s, but also much wider contemporary struggles around housing and racialised housing displacement and deprivation now.

Many of the people included in these accounts have gone on to live active political lives after the events of the squatters' movement. Some of them have been involved in activities that seem incongruent with their squatter activism of the 1970s, sometimes in difficult and challenging ways. I felt it was important not to edit anyone out of this history on the basis of objections I have with their post-squatter actions or activity. This was not an easy decision, and it is not one I feel entirely at peace with, but it is how I chose to navigate the difficulties of working with a recent history where people and events sit close to who and where we are now.

Chapter One begins by setting the broader historical scene and highlights the long relationship between Britain and India, in particular Britain and Sylhet. It relates some of the less well-known history of Sylhet as part of the East India Company's success and how the labour of Sylheti seamen, often referred to as 'lascars', enabled the British Raj to grow its economic and political power at home and abroad in the nineteenth century. This has particular significance since one of the key arguments used to counter the claims of migrant communities to Britain's social resources such as housing is that they are outsiders who have made little to no contribution to the wealth or welfare system of Britain. Entitlement to social housing is thus framed around discourses of indigeneity and belonging, as well as a narrative about Britain's wealth that relies on obscuring the role of Empire. This chapter also looks at the context of the 1970s more closely. It outlines the post-war conditions of migration for Bengali men and the shifting demographics of that community as more and more families begin to join them. It highlights the wider squatter movements that emerged in the face of a growing housing crisis and the tentative connections that emerged with other racially marginalised communities. I also introduce the role of *Race Today* and the Black Power movement that centred on Railton Road in

Brixton and their support for the direct action they saw emerging in the East End community.

Chapter Two looks more directly to the beginnings of the Bengali squatters' movement. It highlights the hardship that Bengali families experienced in obtaining adequate housing and how they took inspiration from white squatter communities by occupying empty properties in the area, many of which were in Dickensian conditions. I outline how individual acts of squatting began to accumulate and, with support from Black Power activists in the *Race Today* collective, formed the basis of a more well-organised movement through the creation of the Bengali Housing Action Group (BHAG). In this chapter, I look at the squatted home as a site of struggle and focus on how the doors and windows of the squatted home became thresholds between the Bengali squatters and the state and street racism they encountered. It was these encounters, either the conversations with the estate managers who implemented the state's racist housing policy or the violent intrusion of street racism that would regularly breach the doors and windows, which in many ways epitomised the battle to belong in 1970s East London. The role of female squatters and their activity as the primary defenders against state and street encroachment is also drawn out here, in acknowledgement that even where partial accounts from this period exist, most often Bengali women's voices were either silenced or omitted.

Chapter Three explores the wider reach of the Bengali squatters' movement outside of the squatted home and examines the development of vigilante groups that connected to a wider homemaking effort in the neighbourhood. I explore how the rural Bengali homemaking imaginary is helpful in explaining how Bengali squatters were not satisfied with simply taking a squatted house but also wanted to recreate something of the homeliness of *para* through vigilantism in the racially hostile neighbourhood. I discuss the development of vigilante groups as a bid to create safety around the squatted community in the absence of police and state protection. I also explore vigilantism as a gendered and generational experience, linking back to the political inheritance of the 1971 Liberation War. I highlight how this generational tension – where younger migrants were willing to fight, but older migrants cautioned for restraint – was misrepresented by popular accounts at the time and was used to service racialised tropes about Bengali effeminacy and passivity.

In Chapter Four I look at how the squatters' movement pressed for and won concessions from the GLC and Tower Hamlets Council and eventually secured tenancies for squatter families. I consider how ambitions differed between those who were part of the more radical elements of BHAG connected to *Race Today* and those who were fighting on narrower terms. This chapter also explores trans-national connections more fully, investigating the links between the homes migrant squatters made here and those they imagined they would return to there. The Sylheti home imaginary revolved not just around dwellings and place but was also deeply nourished by family relationships. The strength of those connections was important to how Bengali migrants approached homemaking between here and there. In establishing the contours of these relationships and how they impacted on attitudes and activism in Spitalfields, I pay particular attention to the importance of ageing, generation and gender.

In the final chapter, I reflect on the relationship between the squatters' struggles in 1970s East London and contemporary issues that shape the experience of Bengali communities in East London. Through interviews with grassroots activists and young people in Tower Hamlets now, I explore how recent processes of residential and commercial gentrification have impacted on, and are being resisted by, the local working-class Bengali community. Since March 2020 Covid-19 has highlighted ongoing inequities in housing, with overcrowding contributing directly to the disproportionate impact of Covid-19 related deaths on the Bengali community in the East End. The intergenerational impact of these changes, and the pressure on traditional familial relationships of care that are exacted by overcrowding and lack of social housing has, in many cases, created displacement away from Tower Hamlets. By focusing on the Save Brick Lane campaign, a coalition that has emerged in response to a proposed new development of the Truman Brewery site on Brick Lane, I highlight how some of the earlier struggles are being revived, while also exploring some of the challenges of organising across complex community ambitions and needs.

This book marks something of a turning point for me personally. I hadn't planned to return to studying or to do the PhD which forms the basis of the research presented here. I imagined I was picking up a community responsibility and that once I had collected interviews and found some way of sharing them, I would resume life as normal. Over three difficult years I completed the PhD at Queen Mary University while juggling reduced teaching hours at a sixth form college and parenting two young children. My fieldwork coincided with the start of the Covid-19 pandemic. The world became a different place for everyone as we managed the restrictions that came with the public health measures, or the hardship that came with sickness, isolation and bereavement. Inevitably, the people I met and the stories I heard refused to remain on the periphery of my life – I realise now that I was foolish to imagine they would. I have chosen to share some of these research and reflection processes in the book, at the start of each chapter.

This book does not claim to be an authoritative account of the Bengali squatters' movement, but rather one contribution to what should be a much richer historical tapestry. It is not possible, nor for me is it desirable, to capture the complexity of the events, the diversity of experiences and the differences of opinion that came to emerge as part of this process in one single piece of work. The Bengali community of the 1970s may have shared similar experiences of housing deprivation and racism, but they certainly are not a homogenous group in either their recollections of these events or indeed their reflections now. For this reason, there will inevitably be stories that were left out, people that were not credited sufficiently and details that have been mis-remembered. I see this as an honest reflection of the messiness of writing and recording complex radical histories and ongoing struggles. I hope that it will inspire a much wider collective effort to recover similar stories.

NOTES

1 I choose to use the term 'Bengali' to describe the mainly Sylheti Bangladeshi community that feature in this book; some writers choose to be more specific and use the term 'Sylheti' whilst others use the term 'Bangladeshi', but in my everyday description of myself and

my community I tend to use Bengali, and I have decided to reflect
that here.

2 I use the term 'racialised' throughout the book to describe the processes by which Bengali migrants, like other migrant groups, were
ascribed a specific racial identity and alienated in that process. As a
verb, 'racialise' points to the fact that 'racial' identities are not derived
from 'factual' or objective scientific knowledge, but rather derived in
a manufactured process that is temporally and geographically located,
and inscribed with exclusionary power. See Nadine El Enany, *(B)
ordering Britain: Law, Race and Empire,* Manchester University Press:
Manchester, 2020.

3 Dan Bulley, Jenny Edkins, Nadine El-Enany (eds), *After Grenfell:
Violence, Resistance and Response,* Pluto Press: London, 2019.

4 Georgie Wemyss, 'White Memories, White Belonging: Competing
Colonial Anniversaries in 'Postcolonial' East London', *Sociological
Research Online,* Vol. 13(5), 2008, pp50-67.

5 The 'here' and 'there' framework sits within what is known as a 'transnational' perspective in geography and migration studies. From this
perspective identities are shaped and defined by attachment to more
than one place. It emerged as a way to think about migration not
just as a one-way journey from one place or 'origin' to another 'destination', but as an ongoing and negotiated identity that often retains
emotional, physical and material connection to two or more places
simultaneously. See for example Steven Vertovec, 'Transnationalism
and identity', *Journal of Ethnic and Migration Studies,* Vol. 27, No. 4,
2001, pp573-582.

6 The term *Londoni* is often used to describe those Bengali migrants
who reside in London (or any part of the UK), who have acquired
elevated status and wealth, by those who did not or were unable to
migrate. *Londoni* homes are built with remittance money and are
usually conspicuously bigger and grander than those of the non-
migrant community.

7 Alison Blunt and Robyn Dowling, *Home,* Routledge: London, 2022.

8 Alexander Vasudevan, *The Autonomous City: A History of Urban
Squatting,* Verso: London, 2017.

9 Hans Pruijt, 'The logic of urban squatting', *International Journal of
Urban and Regional Research,* Vol. 37, 2013, pp19-45.

10 Nick Wates and Christian Wolmar (eds), *Squatting: The Real Story,*
Bay Leaf Books: London, 1980.

1

Shah Jalal: From Sylheti
saint to East End café

A s a young child in the mid 1990s I went on a family trip to
Bangladesh. As a large family of seven children these trips were
irregular, so this was a momentous occasion. My parents are from
Sylhet, and we spent our time between our *basha* (town house)
based in Sylhet town and their natal villages, located further out in
rural areas. This *basha* was significantly bigger and grander than the
house that we lived in London. It had been built from scratch with
the remittance monies that my parents had saved by working long
hours in restaurant kitchens and hunched over industrial sewing
machines. Starting life as a plot of land with dreams of an eventual
return home, the *basha* had become home to extended non-migrant
family, some of whom were not thrilled by the fanfare arrival of the
Londoni entourage. The basha had three levels and several stand-
alone flats. The main section, which we inhabited, had been
designed with upright commodes to facilitate our *Londoni* toilet
habits and had painfully temperamental air conditioning. That
summer, me and my siblings spent long, hot days on the balconies
and the roof terrace, staring across at all the other Londoni *bashas*
in this up-market part of Sylhet. The memories of this trip that are
lodged in my mind oscillate between rushed family visits and hours
sprawled out under ceiling fans as our parents talked in that loud
and animated way that is Bengali habit, cooking and eating, relaxing
in a way that they never did in London.

One of my most vivid memories of this time was a trip we made
to Shah Jalal's *Dargah* (tomb). Shah Jalal was a saint who arrived in

fourteenth-century Sylhet and brought a wave of Islamic conversion to an otherwise mixed Hindu, Buddhist and nascent Muslim population. The visit to the *Dargha* remains etched in my mind because, though as a teenager I had experienced and witnessed poverty and hardship in London, this visit showcased the stark economic inequalities in Sylhet. There were the 'wealthy' *Londonis* like my family – who were rich, regardless of the relative poverty we experienced in London – who arrived in (poorly) air-conditioned vans and visited the Dargah to offer our *duas* (prayers) and charitable donations. Inside the *Dargah* site, though it was busy, it was also calm and reverent. I vaguely remember staring down into the ponds, spying catfish who, legend had it, were the 'black magicians' that Shah Jalal had transformed into fish as punishment for their collusion with the Hindu king. For my parents, this was an important spiritual visit, an opportunity to express gratitude and give charity as repayment for all their blessings. For me, it was a brutal exposure to extreme poverty; although the site itself was ordered and well managed, outside surrounding the *Dargha* were throngs of destitute men, women and children, offering their deformed and mutilated bodies to the *Londoni* gaze, pleading with the spiritual visitors for money. Those encounters with poverty at the Shah Jalal *Dargah* and the contrast with remittance 'rich' visitors to the site was an early lesson in the violence of global capitalism and the inequalities it generates. In part for this reason, Shah Jalal's *Dargah* is also a useful node from which to trace the complex geographies and long histories that underpin the Bengali squatters' movement.

THE SHAH JALAL CONNECTION

Sylhet is about 300 miles northeast of Calcutta and a similar distance to the Chinese border. Bangladesh shares its longest land border with India and is nearly 1400 miles from Pakistan, of which it was one wing when the latter was carved out during the partition of India in 1947. Although parts of Sylhet are hilly, it is, broadly speaking, 6000 square kilometres of flat land, which are often deeply flooded during the rainy season. The riverine geographies of the land have played an important part in Sylhet's history and development. During periods of conquest, the hillier areas proved to be a troublesome frontier for those who wanted to exert uniform control, while the flat lowland area, with a more settled agricultural population, were more persuadable to power shifts and change.

In the early fourteenth century, a Muslim saint by the name of Shah Jalal and his 360 travelling *awliyas* (disciples) arrived in what was known as *Silhat*. There are various early accounts of Shah Jalal's life and travels, including records in the famous Moroccan Muslim traveller Ibn Battutah's travelogues, where he notes meeting him in 1346. Though most traditional knowledge locates Shah Jalal's 'roots' in Yemen, there is also a suggestion that he was probably from Turkestan and later moved to Yemen.

Shah Jalal had left Mecca with a fistful of soil handed to him by his maternal uncle, who instructed him to go forth and spread Islam and to settle only where the soil matched that which he had been given. He was a well-respected Sufi mystic and the story goes that Shah Jalal's travels led him to travel to Sylhet and help over-throw the Hindu King, Gaur Govinda, in the 1340s. He tested the soil he had travelled with and found that the soil of Sylhet matched the fistful he carried: he and his followers settled. They were sent out across Sylhet to marry and 'root' down new Muslim commu-nities, and while a sizeable Hindu population remained, Sylhet became a majority Muslim area.

In 1346 the famous traveller Ibn Battuta wrote about making his way across the subcontinent to pay Shah Jalal a visit. Ibn Battuta's travel writings are important because, though much of this story is collected through oral tradition, and no doubt much has been added for dramatic effect, many of the facts of Shah Jalal's arrival to Sylhet relate to both people and events that are historically authoritative. The journeys of Shah Jalal and Ibn Battuta are also an important reminder that, in the context of tracing this history, ideas of indi-geneity and bounded place contradict the realities of mobility of people and interaction between places. The idea of roots/routes, which Paul Gilroy talks about in his book *The Black Atlantic*, is embedded in the development of a Sylheti identity that has been sedimented through mobility and migration for hundreds of years.[1]

The story of Shah Jalal as captured by other Muslim travellers and traders tell us something about the heritage of Sylhet and speaks to the broader idea that cultural exchange and mobility has long been part of our history. It enables us to think about diasporic communities as not solely generated by twentieth-century conditions, but to recognise the complex web of interactions that reaches back well before the British link that was to come. One of the interesting contributions of Ibn Battuta is his observation that Sylhetis, even in the fourteenth century, were renowned for their boat building. As a region of riverscapes, trade and travel were reliant on boats and he noted a specific boat building tradition using timber from the abundant forests of Sylhet. Ashfaque Hossain, a Dhaka University historian, notes that Ibn Battuta's diaries record significant trade routes between Sylhet and East Asia even at that time, which points to a Sylheti sailing lineage that predates earlier accounts.[2] This observation is also made by Robert Lindsay, who arrived some 400 years later in 1777, making his way up the Meghna from Calcutta by boat.

LINDSAY AND THE LIMESTONE

In the centuries that followed Ibn Battuta's visit, Shah Jalal's *Dargah* became a source of legitimation for other 'visitors' and, in tandem, also a site for resistance. The British arrived not with Shah Jalal's desire for settlement and proselytising, but with a ledger for maximum value extraction. However, even they noted that the act of paying public respect to Shah Jalal's *Dargah* was a necessary gesture for appeasing the local power elites before they brought Sylhet, Bengal and the rest of the subcontinent under imperial control.

Robert Lindsay was born to the Earl of Balcarres and Anne Dalrymple in Scotland in 1754. He was put under the stewardship of his maternal uncle who was a merchant, travelling to Cádiz with him and later securing a role in a shipping office. Some years later, in 1772, he relates leaving for a clerical role in the revenue department of the East India Company, travelling under the Captaincy of a Welshman with only one arm for a voyage of some six months, before coming into the mouth of the Hoogly River.

In Lindsay's account, *Anecdotes of an Indian Life*, he describes coming into Calcutta thus:

In approaching the town of Calcutta, nothing can be more beautiful or have a finer effect than the appearance of the banks, everywhere studded with country villas, covered with beautiful verdure, and resembling the best cultivated counties of England,—very different from what one would expect to find under a vertical sun. The continual succession of ships, from all nations, passing up and down, enlivens the scene, and gives the most delightful prospect to a stranger after a long and tedious voyage.[3]

From there he travelled by river boat, navigating the Sunderbans through thick forests 'inhabited only by tigers, alligators and wild animals', noting, 'it is a dreary waste of great extent, but beautiful in the extreme', before arriving and settling in Dhaka.[4] It was in a chance conversation with a retiring revenue collector that Lindsay learned about the profitability of a company post in Sylhet and, with shrewd manoeuvring, describes raising himself from a relatively low clerical position to successor for this post, ahead of senior and more experienced officers.

Seven days of river journeying brought him into the Surma River that runs through Sylhet. Soon after his arrival, he recalls being informed that it was customary practice that new 'residents' pay their respects to the 'tutelar saint Shaw Jullol' – so Shah Jalal's Shah Jalal's *Dargah*, the site of Shah Jalal's tomb and his last resting place, became today's equivalent of a 'virtue signalling' event; Lindsay reports that he proceeded with diligent haste, 'as others had done before me, left my shoes on the threshold and deposited on the tomb five gold mohurs as an offering'.[5]

From here on Lindsay took up his position as Revenue Collector and embarked on various speculative trade opportunities. He realised the commercial opportunities in Sylhet's *chunam* (limestone) in the hills above Chattak, the area of my father's natal village. His account of monopolising the trade of limestone records the existence of Greeks, Armenians and other 'low Europeans', who were already busy extracting limestone in these hilly areas – in his efforts to secure a monopoly, he reports going to meet the chieftains of the area and describes the setting of their meeting as one of the most 'stupendous amphitheatres in the world'.[6]

Despite what he describes as their 'fierce' appearance, Lindsay negotiated access to the limestone hills and a favourable spot for his boats. Within a few months he had established an entire fleet of boats and, with 500-600 men in his employment, began an enormously profitable trade in limestone. That limestone was transported by river boats and was used for 'building the fort and rising city of Calcutta'.[7] Lindsay also noted the significant wealth generated by the capture and trading of elephants, reporting that he caught and traded at least five hundred for every one of his twelve years in Sylhet. These were highly lucrative income streams, in addition to his Revenue Collector's salary.

Lindsay's journey to Sylhet was not navigated by a spiritually guided fistful of soil, and he left with a fortune the size of which, even he confesses, he had not dreamed of attaining. Unlike Shah Jalal, who settled and made a home, Lindsay endorsed with earnest conviction the fear that, staying for too long, 'we should eventually lose our character and intrepidity, which alone supports our name in India'.[8] For Lindsay, there was never intention to settle; the route to Sylhet and back was a financial contract and one that delivered so abundantly that he was able to purchase the family home from his older brother.

Balcarres House in Fife, Scotland.

Balcarres House, nestled in the southern Fifeshire countryside, nowhere attests to the Sylheti labour or limestone that were integral to its retention in the family and its subsequent developments. This is not unusual for colonial-era property acquisition; indeed, it represents the way in which colonially derived wealth is ritually absorbed into, and obscured by, the fabric of British society.

Lindsay's wealth – generated by the appropriation of the labour and natural resources of Sylhet – may have been diverted to Fifeshire in rural Scotland, but as an employee of the East India Company, whose first office and warehouse were based in Leadenhall Street, it was to the City of London, the UK's financial heart, that the money was primarily flowing. Leadenhall Street is only a mile away from Brick Lane, the area now described as the heartland of the Bengali diaspora in the UK. Bengali migration to East London may be temporally fixed to the post-war migration period in the popular national imagination. However, this involves a significant erasure of both the earlier East India Company connection and the hundreds of years of maritime migrant connection between Sylhet and Spitalfields that opened the later migrant network.

Shah Jalal's legacy travelled with the Bengali sailors who toiled in the bellies of the English mercantile ships to London, where his name was invoked in one of the first East End cafés opened on Commercial Street in the 1920s. The Shah Jalol Café, along with other such establishments, led to the development of the 'Indian restaurant' trade, which became an important source of business and employment for Bengali migrants in the post-war period. Shah Jalal's fistful of soil had navigated him on a divine mission to Sylhet, but in that unpredictable entanglement of roots/routes, his name ended up gracing a Spitalfields café serving Sylheti migrants in East London some 700 years later.

SHAH JALOL'S SAILORS

Shah Jalol Café was opened on 76 Commercial Street by ex-seaman Ayub Ali in the 1920s. It evidences an earlier community of Sylheti sailors, some of whom are featured in the collection of oral histories *Across Seven Seas and Thirteen Rivers: Life Stories of Pioneer Sylheti*

Settlers in Britain. The author, Caroline Adams, was a youth and community worker in the East End in the late 1970s and 1980s and enjoyed something approaching honorary Bengali status for the value of her community work and the archival contribution it generated.[9]

Caroline spent time travelling in India and ventured to Bangladesh at the dawn of its independence. In London she worked in various community-facing services in the East End and became fluent in Bengali. She was able to engage with the migrant community in a way that unsettled the insider/outsider dichotomy usually constructed between researchers and respondents. Her work is remarkable for the stories she was able to solicit and collect. In many of Caroline's interviews, Ayub Ali is described by her participants as critical to their early settlement in London.

Ayub Ali was born in the 1880s in Sylhet. He left Sylhet before the First World War as a sailor. Little is known about the circumstances of that journey except that he arrived in London having 'jumped ship' in the US and somehow made his way to East London. It was here that, along with his brother who arrived at approximately the same time, Ayub Ali opened the seamen's café on 76 Commercial Street. In homage to their Sylheti roots, they called it the Shah Jalol Café. This café became the site of the community's political organising, including hosting meetings for the India League, an organisation that campaigned and fundraised for an independent India.

As Rozina Visram notes in her book *Asians in Britain: 400 Years of History*, Ayub Ali was given the title 'Master' (teacher) as a signal of how esteemed his contributions were to this inter-war Bengali community.[10] Shah Jalol Café was not just an eatery and place for political gathering but a space of refuge and support. Like many other cafes and boarding houses, usually in dock areas near major ports, it was a bridging institution, 'which offered succour to the newcomer'.[11] Ayub Ali was celebrated by many of Caroline Adams's participants for helping them deal with the bureaucracy of India House and the police. As sailors or ex-sailors, there were significant contractual and immigration obligations imposed on the seamen, many of whom were unable to read or write English. He supported them from Shah Jalol Café and from Number 13 Sandys House, also in Spitalfields, a property he came to own, which became a boarding house for Sylheti sailors as they found their feet in London.

One of the interviewees in Caroline Adams's work recalled with some humour the occasion of a Bengali woman visiting the Shah Jalol Café. The interviewee, Shah Abdul Majid Qureshi, remembered that the woman had arrived at the café with her husband, who had been a soldier in the Second World War. Upon entering the café, she insisted that she was so deprived of Bengali female company that she needed to converse with some of her own women, and so rushed straight into the kitchen. She returned moments later, flustered and alarmed, upon realising that the kitchen was staffed by men. The story, though recounted with amusement, is some indication of the loneliness that the few Bengali migrant women arriving in Britain at that time must have experienced.[12]

Sylheti men were employed initially as ship workers and servants by the East India Company and then on English imperial naval and commercial vessels docking near Canning Town. There is no simple answer to why the Indian seamen community came to be dominated by Sylheti men given the distance of Sylhet from any major port. However, Ashfaque Hossain argues that we can find credible explanation in the earlier boat-building and navigating traditions of Sylhet that both Ibn Battuta and Robert Lindsay comment upon in their accounts.[13]

A significant part of Lindsay's biography celebrates his boat-building ventures, claiming 'we became ... in great repute as elegant boatbuilders'. He recalls a letter from his mother entreating him, 'I understand, my dear Robert, that you are a great ship-builder – your talents in this line I do not dispute – but I have one favour to ask of you, which is, that you will not come home in one of your own building'.[14] The shipbuilding tradition in Sylhet was critical to the wealth that the British government was able to extract from the region. Ashfaque Hossain notes that total exports in the 1870s were valued at £597,000 and the bulk of that had moved away from the limestone that had made Robert Lindsay's personal fortune to the export of tea, grown in the hillier areas in the north-east. Hossain notes that before the advent of the railways, the boat system from Sylhet to Calcutta offered the British enormous commercial gains.[15]

Administratively, Sylhet's prominent commercial position was part of the reason it was annexed from Bengal into Assam, with significant consequences for the way the British revenue collection system impacted on land tenure for Sylhetis. By the late nineteenth century, emerging transport systems in the form of river steamers and the construction of railways lines created a newer export destination in the port of Chittagong. The impact of this shift away from traditional boat employment, directed by British export and commercial interest, is one of the key reasons that Hossain argues Sylheti boatmen began to seek employment outside of the riverscapes they had traditionally navigated, turning to employment in seagoing ships.

The annexation of Sylhet to Assam also indirectly contributed to this pivot towards the sea. The British had, by the 1870s, recognised the enormous commercial potential for tea cultivation in the hillier areas of Sylhet to complement the burgeoning tea trade in the neighbouring district of Assam. They used the annexation to bring the Assamese and Sylheti tea plantation system into a coherent and financially viable administrative district. In taking this decision they ignored local protests, which claimed that Sylhet was historically, culturally and linguistically an integral part of Bengal. It was not until 1947, after a referendum in Sylhet, that the region was once again assimilated into Bengal, which would eventually become part of East Pakistan during the partition of India.

Katy Gardner, an anthropologist who has spent decades living and working between Sylhet and London, argues that the annexation led to a different land tenure system in Sylhet, which had significant impact on the maritime connection that developed:

> The political and economic structure laid down by the British in Sylhet was therefore significantly different from other districts. Instead of a small elite of landlords, and a large majority of tenants, much of the rural Sylheti population tended land which, despite the revenues paid to the British, was their own.[16]

This generated a sense of economic autonomy but also created the problem that as the population grew, the subdivisions of land jeopardised the ability of families to remain self-sufficient. Hossain agrees that from the late nineteenth century, this land-based economic stress had the impact of 'leading young and venturesome individuals into the hot engine rooms of merchant ships'.[17] The period of British involvement in Sylhet shifted from the eighteenth-century extraction of raw material and tax collection to nineteenth-century profiteering based on cheap and exploited labour.

In his book *Globalising Labour: Indian Seafarers and World Shipping*, Gopal Balachandran explores the experience of thousands of Indian seafarers who were critical to global commercial enterprise, first at the East India Company and then for the British imperial state:

> Indian seafarers manned decks on the world's ships and crewed engine rooms, saloons, cabins and galleys. They inhabited a world deeply marked by race which determined what they would do, how much they would be paid, and how they could be treated. Virtually until World War II, barring the odd Parsi doctor, junior engineer, or deck officer, officers on European ships were almost all white … The racial divide ran deeper than rank, yet nowhere was it more complete that the engine room where the engineers were all white [and] the Indian crews did the hot and heavy work of heaving coal and stoking the fires.[18]

'Lascar' is the term commonly used to describe these Indian seamen and is believed to have first been used by Portuguese and Dutch mercantile traders to describe Indian seafarers originating from the Indian Ocean area, although it has also been used to describe seamen from the Middle East, China and Africa. There is some evidence to suggest that the term is derived from the Persian term *lashkar*, which means 'an army'. Whatever its origins, the term was absorbed into the legal language of the employment contracts and merchant shipping laws that came to define and dominate the Indian seafarers experience of employment.

The need for Indian seamen first arose because of high levels of sickness, death and desertion on India-bound ships. Rozina Visram notes that 'desertions became more prevalent once sailors attracted by better prospects began to join the armies of Indian princes', leaving ship captains little choice but to recruit Indian sailors – this was not without resistance from the British state; indeed, up until 1802, 'successive British governments forbade the employment of lascars on ships sailing west of the Cape of Good Hope'.[19] Later legislative changes appear to concede to the need to employ Indian seamen, but firmly stipulate that whilst these seamen may be born in territories of the British government, they were not eligible for British sailor standard contracts.

By 1813, and under pressure from merchant capitalists agitating for their share of the spoils of Empire, the British government withdrew the monopoly granted to the East India Company. As Visram highlights, it was 'free trade, coupled with steam power' that eventually meant 'lascars became the mainstay of the labour force in British registered ships bound for Europe'.[20] Balachandran estimates that as early as the 1850s, some 3000 Indian seafarers were sailing to Britain every year. Balachandran and Visram's work give an extensive account of the Indian seamen's connection to Britain, revealing the conditions of that experience, the seamen's critical value to Britain's imperial capabilities and the financial gains achieved from their work.

The National Archives house the Registrar of Shipping and Seamen, a register of ships and seamen that was established following the 1835 Merchant Shipping Act. Though this centralised system ceased from 1857-1914, in the interim period crew lists and agreements were recorded. For ships involved in foreign trade, these records were submitted at the end of each voyage.

The crew list for the ship Duke Buccleuch records the seamen that worked a voyage departing from Calcutta port on 14 December 1880, which docked in London on the 31 January 1881. The list details the forty-nine seamen originating variously from Calcutta, 'Dacca' and Chittagong. Sixteen of them of them identify their place of birth in 'Silhet'. They are employed in various roles but most of them are listed as 'firemen' working in the ship's coal-fired furnaces. The youngest of these men was 24-year-old Abdool Rohomon, who is recorded as having worked this same ship and voyage previously. Other ships like the Duke of Devonshire, which also recorded a voyage in 1881, have lists of crew members who were mainly from 'Silhet'. There, the oldest sailor was Sameer, aged forty, who was also identified as having made this voyage before.

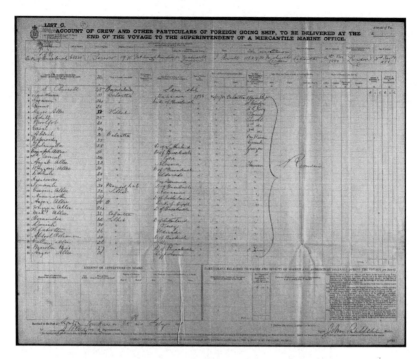

Ship register of Duke Buccleuch dated 1881, at the
National Archives Library.

These 'Silheti' seamen would have been signed on to inferior work
contracts that became known as 'Asiatic articles'. These contracts
were directly discriminatory in the employment terms and conditions offered, paying between one-fifth and one-third the pay of the
European sailors on the same ship. At the same time, the contract
stipulated that lascars were denied permission to stay in England
and had to ensure that they worked a return passage home. On the
ship, the lives of sailors were challenging. Caroline Adams writes:

> With the introduction of steam, the companies came to rely
> still more on Indian seamen who were held to be more suit-
> able as engine-room crews than British seamen as they were
> used to high temperatures and could therefore withstand the
> appalling heat suffered by firemen stoking furnaces under a
> steel deck on the Arabian sea ... Some men died of heat stroke
> and exhaustion, others overcome with heat threw themselves
> overboard in desperation.[21]

Shah Abdul Majid Qureshi, quoted earlier quipping about the Bengali woman at Shah Jalol's café, remembered:

> I was called a bunkerman. In the coal bunker ... it was hot, oh yes, it was hot. We put coal in the boiler and then it gets heat and then the ship runs. It is a most difficult job, very hard and very hot too – many people died in that heat. In my sea life, I knew hundreds of people that died.[22]

The brutal work conditions described contrast starkly with the representation of lascars in archive images.

Three Lascars of the 'Viceroy of India' (1929) standing behind the wheel of one of the ship's tender. Waterline Collection, National Maritime Musuem, London.

The preceding image is featured on the the National Maritime Museum's 'Lascars and the East India Company' landing page and is one that is regularly featured in popular and academic papers about Indian sailors. The image is entitled 'Three Indian sailors on the Viceroy of India', a ship which was P&O's flagship cruise liner before being sunk during the Second World War. The photograph was taken by the Marine Photo Service. Heloise Finch-Boyer explores how this Essex-based photographic company was employed to take photographs that would then be bought as souvenirs by cruise-liner passengers. She notes how the Indian seamen (they are believed to be from northern India, not Sylhet) were clothed in uniforms that distinguish them from the white sailors. These uniforms, with their *topi* (headgear) and belts, were used to identify different ship roles. Her archival research has led her to interrogate the colonial gaze evident in images like these, where the Indian seamen are represented as 'exoticised figures'.[23] The purpose of the photograph is not to record or identify individuals, but 'to enable souvenir collectors to display their tourist experiences'; she goes on to note how other images and uniforms are used to reinforce 'existing perceptions of racial difference around notions of manliness and effeminacy' in contrast to white sailors, who are always depicted in 'hyper-masculine poses of independence and confidence, topped off with their caps worn at jaunty angles'.[24]

Gopal Balachandran argues that the 'vast silences that fill official records about Indian seafarers' lives are like the inanities that often passed for official knowledge, not without meaning'; he highlights the 'unevenness in source materials', for example 'reams of minutes and notes' that 'pore minutely over whether Indian seafarers should be allowed coffee in their diets'.[25] Heloise Finch-Boyle uses ship-plans to investigate some of these absences. These plans verify, for instance, that South Asian crew and European crew areas were segregated, and that South Asian crew members were, before 1914, entitled to no more than one cubic metre of accommodation space. This means that the crew listed in the Duke of Bucculeuch and the Duke of Devonshire were confined to significantly more cramped bunks than their European counterparts. The rations that were accorded to seamen were also dictated by strict measures that were calculated and reviewed in minute detail by the government in consultation with shipowners, and were also substantially more frugal in quality and quantity than for their white peers. Records indicate that these rations were subjected to bitter disputes and petitions, in addition to demands for larger berths.[26] In fact, Aaron Jaffer claims that the strict segregation and regular shortages of food on voyages sometimes became both the subject of and medium through which mutinies came about:

> Severe shortages of food and water could precipitate the most serious forms of mutiny. Lascars belonging to the Lark (1783), accused Captain Dean of denying them food during the vessels voyage along the Coromandel Coast. One man claimed that Dean had 'stinted the usual allowance of provisions and water to the crew, which induced them to consult about throwing the captain overboard as being tired of passing so disagreeable a life'. The third mate of the Asia (1813) claimed that the contentious issue of water rations had been raised by the crew several times before a group of seacunnies murdered the captain. He reported that 'the serang with the tindal had joined [the mutineers] in a remonstrance on the preceding day – they complained the captain that their allowance of water was small, while the captain and the rest drank what they chose'.[27]

South Asian crew had separate kitchen galley areas for their Hindu and Muslim seamen and this also meant that one of the roles often performed by Indian seamen was the position of ship's cook. Rozina Visram notes that the 'Indian restaurant' and British appetite for curry, most noted since the 1960s, is in fact rooted in the galleys of these ships and the Sylheti galley cooks during this period.[28] Merchant shipping laws required seamen to possess a 'Certificate of Competency in Cooking' in order to perform the role of ship-cook and various other galley duties. The certificate below was found in the Caird Library at the National Maritime Museum in Greenwich, London. The certificate gives a 'Rhhim Bux' (probably Rohim Baksh) born in 1907 in Sylhet, son of Nawab Meah, the legal certification he needed to perform his cook's duties. It was men like this in the early twentieth century that were in the Shah Jalol Café kitchen, giving respite and some 'home comfort' through the provision of curry and rice to the growing number of seamen who were 'jumping ship' and pursuing better employment prospects outside of the shipping industry in the post-war period.

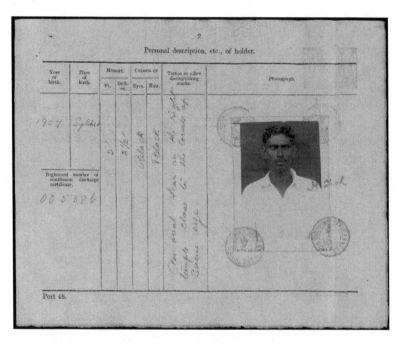

Colonial Cooks Certificate issued to Rhhim Bux. Year of Birth 1907. Place of Birth Sylhet © Crown Copyright. National Maritime Museum, London.

The legal status of these Sylheti seamen would have been complex and shares some commonalities with those impacted by the Windrush scandal, who had arrived as British subjects in the 1940s but found their citizenship status questioned – and in many cases revoked – decades later. Georgie Wemyss describes the way in which 'working class Indian seafarers faced considerable barriers in settling in Britain ... thereby producing their invisibility in national narratives and maintaining the idea of the British nation as white'.[29] There was an armature of legal writ and bordering practices that enabled the cheap labour provided by Indian seamen, but which simultaneously sought to exclude them from permanent settlement in the UK.

In the nineteenth century, on ships like the Duke Buccleuch and the Duke of Devonshire, Indian seamen were sometimes not permitted to land at all, and by 1894 the Merchant Shipping Act gave ship owners the power to compel Indian seamen to leave via vessels heading back to India, even if they didn't have a work contract. Wemyss challenges the term 'jumping ship', suggesting that, 'apart from suicide', it was the 'only escape from the all-encompassing control of the shipping companies'.[30] For those that did leave the ships in-between voyages, the duty on the East India Company to provide the Indian seamen with board and provisions until the next voyage home was often neglected and led to concerns as early as the eighteenth century about the numbers of destitute lascars in and around the docks of East London. Caroline Adams writes:

> By the end of the Napoleonic wars there were as many as 1,100 lascars in London at any time and they were allocated a barracks at Gravesend. The death rate in winter in the barracks became known to the Asiatic Society and an angry letter to *The Times* led to a Parliamentary enquiry.[31]

With the decline of the East India Company and the emergence of competitive shipping companies, even this meagre provision was neglected:

> By the 1840s the situation had become so scandalous that the Reverend Henry Venn and Joseph Salter of the Church Missionary Society, felt moved to undertake an investigation into the condition of the destitute seamen and ex-seamen living in lodging houses and hovels around Cable Street ...[32]

In one incident alone, forty Indian seamen were found dead after a cold winter's night in East London. In 1858, after a fundraising campaign that made claim to 'good Christian conscience', the Strangers Home for Asiatics, Africans and South Sea Islanders was opened, with 200 beds on the West India Dock Road. For some Indian seamen – including, no doubt, many from Sylhet – the Strangers Home would have been their lodgings in the period between their voyages. For others there were also less 'reputable' lodging houses, which also offered 'companionship' with women of equally 'dubious' reputation.[33]

Among those who left their shipping contracts in the 1930s is the recently recovered story of Paku Miah. Paku Miah, highlighted in the National Archives' 'Seafarers Stories', could well have been a sailor from Sylhet. His story has been pieced together from a few different archival sources and through some calibration, it is possible to intimate some of the details of his life as he manages to outwit and escape the institutions that attempted to send him back to India.

Paku appears first in the archives in letters between the Office of the High Commissioner of India and the ship owners, when he is accused of deserting his ship *SS Inanda* at West India Docks in June 1931. Here the concern is about locating his whereabouts, and a statement is issued clarifying that any financial costs for his support were the obligation of the ship owner. The ship owners reply to say that he had disappeared from the Strangers Home for Asiatics and report they will endeavour to recover him through police assistance. The police do manage to track him down at an address in Spitalfields in December 1931. In a letter dated 28 January 1932 it is reported that he was prosecuted under section 224 of the Merchant Shipping Act 1894 and made to pay a penalty, which was 'forfeiture of wages which amounted to £3.10 and also directed that he should be conveyed back to his ship under police escort'.[34] However, the letter goes on to state that Paku Miah arrived at the ship and remained defiant; his name was not under any contract or articles for a return voyage and because he flatly refused to sign any new contract for that return voyage, the letter states that 'the Master of the Officers of the vessel had no authority whatever to prevent him from going ashore, which he eventually did as he said he would to the Police which escorted him aboard.'[35]

COPY.   THE SHIPPING FEDERATION LIMITED.

52,Leadenhall Street,
London,E.C.3.

Messrs.Thos.& Jas.Harrison,   28th January,1932
  Mersey Chambers,
  Liverpool.

Dear Sirs:

PAKU MIAH ex "INANDA"

       I am in receipt of your letter of the 26th inst.with
copy of a letter received from the High Commissioner for India
relating to the above-named Indian Seaman.
       On instructions received from your London Office we
prosecuted this man in London on the 3rd December last,proceedings
being taken against him under Section 224 of the Merchant Shipping
Act 1894. Although the summons which was directed for service at
the address which was given by the High Commissioner for India,
namely, 52, Worship Street,Finsbury,E.C.2 we had great difficulty,
however, in finding the man, but eventually the Police succeeded in
tracing him to an address in Spitalfields,E. The Magistrate at the
Thames Police Court having found the defendant guilty made an order
for the forfeiture of wages which amounted to £3.10.0. and also
directed that he should be conveyed back to his ship,under Police
Escort. This was eventually carried out the same afternoon. This
man not being on the Articles of the "Inanda", and as he definitely
refused to sign same, the master or the Officers of the vessel
had no authority whatever to prevent him from going ashore, which
he eventually did as he said he would to the Police which escorted
him on board.
       I have discussed the matter with our Solicitors to-day
and they confirm the opinion which I previously held that as the
order of the court in question had been complied with, I cannot
see, having regard to the attitude of the man, and that he has
been in a position to maintain himself up to the present, what
further legal steps the Shipowners can take or even the Commissioner
for India to have this Indian seaman removed from the Country.
It must not be overlooked that the Agreement which Paku Miah signed
in India no longer operates as it expired some time ago, and also
that he is a British Subject.

               Yours faithfully,
                Michael Brett,
                Secretary,
               Per A.C.E.(Sgd)

Letter from Shipping Federation Ltd in search of Paku Miah.
January 1932, National Archives.

The last lines of this letter state that Paku is a 'British Subject'
and is telling of the blurry legal status that Sylheti seamen occupied
as part of the British Empire. There are several more letters that run
between the shipping company and India House, which bemoan
the inability of any legal recourse to compel Paku to return to India.
In February 1932 the Home Office remarks that they are 'surprised

how easy it is for a Lascar deserter to defy the clear order of the Court'.[36] In response, the Board of Trade states that they 'cannot suggest any means of compelling this man to return to sea or of sending him back to India against his will'.[37] In March 1932, the India High Commission grants him a 'naturalisation certificate'; this gives him the ability to register for work and rescues him from the precarity of being a registered 'alien', a status derived from the 1919 Aliens Restriction (Amendment) Act, which was part of the legislative framework that Wemyss describes as aimed to 'produce and maintain the material and cultural whiteness of the metropole and settler colonies'.[38]

We know that Paku Miah lived in Spitalfields after he escaped his shipping contract, and he may well have been one of the men that sought out company in Shah Jalol Café on 76 Commercial Street. Indeed, it is possible that he was an associate of, or sought help from, Ayub Ali Master as he engaged in what must have been an extraordinary act of defiance: an Indian seaman refusing the triple injunctions of a powerful shipping company employer, the colonial reach of India House and the criminal justice system. Although the archives do not verify if he was from Sylhet, Paku's story helps to understand something of the presence of these Indian sailors and what so many of those unarchived lives may have been like. Whether he stayed in the East London community of seamen who were likewise finding their own way out of shipping contracts that expected them to toil on ships in discriminatory contracts is unknown.

We also do not know if he became one of the thousands of Indian seamen who were recruited into the Merchant Navy during the Second World War. Hossain reports that during this war, 4,786 merchant ships were lost, with some 32,000 sailors dead. Of those, he estimates that many would have been Sylheti seamen, toiling in the depths of the ship's engine rooms with the least likelihood of escape when under attack.

Nawab Ali, a Second World War veteran interviewed by Caroline Adams, reported:

I was born under the British flag, and I supported Britain ... I was in Port Said when the Queen came there, she was Princess Elizabeth then. I heard what she said. She said, 'Must be we will win this war, and when we do, there will be pensions for everyone who fought.' I am still waiting for my pension. Soon I will write to the Queen about that. Britain wanted us then. I think now people have forgotten about that.[39]

Though the geographies of the Sylheti Bengali migrant community in the East End predates the East India Company's venture into Bengal in the eighteenth century, and the Sylheti seamen that have traversed ports between here and there since, it was after the Second World War that the number of Bengali migrants significantly increased. In 1947, after the partition of India and the creation of Pakistan, Sylheti sailors found themselves cut off from the ship-work they had traditionally been recruited for in Calcutta, which was now a part of India. Sarah Glynn's comparative historical research of East End migrant communities reports that the Pakistani government initially implemented punitive restrictions that made it deliberately more difficult for people in the eastern part of the divided country to secure papers to travel to Britain. After much protest those restrictions were gradually lifted, and by 1962 many thousands of Bengali men, mostly from Sylhet, were migrating to the areas in London and other port cities where earlier Indian seamen had created small communities.[40]

The Bengali migrant community in East London is generally dated to the later post-war period of the 1960s and 1970s, when the invitation to New Commonwealth citizens to migrate and work in Britain led to a steadier stream of single Bengali men arriving to take up positions in the garment factories along Brick Lane, as well as low-paid positions in hotels and catering. These men were not ship-goers – they travelled in planes departing from Dhaka's international airport, which in 1980 was re-named Shah Jalal Airport. Predictably, these newer migrants gravitated to the communities that those earlier migrants had established. They may not have been familiar with the arduous and discriminatory labour practices of the merchant ships, but they too became part of a cheap migrant labour force, this time on land.

Most of the men who arrived during this period were young and had little intention of staying. Katy Gardner describes those single migrant men as 'transnationals par excellence' who had 'every intention of returning to the homeland once enough money had been accrued'.[41] Unlike the Sylheti seamen, advances in aviation made return journeys home more readily accessible, and many men spent decades commuting between Sylhet and Spitalfields with little desire or ambition to settle. Most of these men lived in multiple occupancy houses, privately renting from Jewish land-lords who had in many cases recently moved out of the East End themselves, or from the odd Bengali migrant who had managed to buy one of the cheaper properties in and around Spitalfields, like Ayub Ali.

Ironically, it was growing anti-immigration sentiment that led to the legislative changes which arguably shifted this initial transnational commuting tradition towards increasing family settlement in the UK. By 1962 the Commonwealth Immigration Act was restricting the numbers of 'coloured immigrants' into Britain from so-called New Commonwealth countries following the racist violence (and subsequent resistance) that broke out in 1958 across cities in the UK, including Notting Hill in London and Nottingham. With these changes, Bengali migrants now had to demonstrate that they were in possession of a 'work voucher' and that they were coming to take up a specific job.

Following concerted anti-racist campaigning by African, Asian and Caribbean communities in Britain led by figures like Claudia Jones in London, the mid 1960s saw the creation of the Race Relations Act to outlaw direct racialised discrimination. However, this was undermined by sustained efforts to further restrict immi-gration, which fed racist narratives by promoting the view that 'coloured immigrants' were a threat to the British polity. In the wake of Enoch Powell's 'Rivers of Blood' speech, the clamour for further restrictions led to the 1971 Immigration Act, which, instead of relying on work vouchers, restricted immigration to family dependency. It was, in many ways, the restrictions imposed by this law that catalysed the biggest wave of family re-unification migration for the Bengali community, and which created one of the critical conditions of the 1970s Bengali squatters' movement.

Throughout the 1960s and 1970s, compelling evidence emerged that in both the public and private sector, ethnic minority commu-nities encountered direct and indirect racism in housing provision in cities across the UK. In 1967 a report by Political and Economic Planning (PEP) concluded that there were serious levels of disadvantage suffered by the 'West Indian applicant', who was refused accommodation or required to pay a higher rent on forty-five out of sixty occasions investigated.[42] In 1975 a Runnymede Trust report also highlighted that minority ethnic communities were living in the worst quality housing stock, both in the public and private sector. Using 1971 census results, they reported that households of New Commonwealth origin were disproportionately concentrated in poor quality housing estates and were living in the most over-crowded conditions.[43]

The Spitalfields Housing and Planning Rights Service (SHPRS) was an important local advice service that specifically looked at racialised discrimination in housing in the borough of Tower Hamlets. Charlie Forman, one of the housing advice workers in this service and a participant in my research, wrote in *Spitalfields: A Battle for Land* that 'in 1966, a third of all adverts in the local press for privately rented rooms actually specified "no coloureds"'.[44] Spitalfields had been excluded from post-war development plans and as a result had an abundance of cheap, privately rented accommodation, generally in poor condition. For migrant communities, the years of residency required to qualify for social housing meant that most of them had no choice but to start their housing journeys in the private sector.

Forman describes in disbelief how the slum conditions that had been criticised by Charles Booth's *Life and Labour of the People in London* were, nearly one hundred years later, being experienced by newly arrived Bengali migrant families:

> No hot water, no inside toilet. No bath. With slight variations. This is how many hundreds of Bangladeshi families were living in the 1970s and even the 1980s. The whole family would sleep in one room and use the other room for cooking, eating and living. In the larger three-room tenements, the family would still normally sleep in one room. With other male relatives sharing the second bedroom, even if there had been the money, there was no space for a bathroom.[45]

He goes on to say that, while overcrowding was one problem, the other was the state of disrepair:

> In the front passageway there is a mass of old metres and wiring. Ahead is the staircase. Several stairs are loose, the plaster on the underside of the stairs is damp and perished. The upstairs toilet leaks. The roof is shot. No one can survive on the top floor. In storms, water find its way all the way down to the ground. There's only one door from the passage to the ground floor rooms, the other has been sealed, so these two rooms have been connected by hacking through the wall dividing them and wedging up a makeshift door frame. A family of seven sleeps in the front room. To fit them in, hardboard has been laid on empty milk crates with mattresses spread across the hardboard. This way the whole family can sleep in one elongated bed, only the baby has its own cot. There is little room for any other furniture. The windows are broken and boarded up. A draught still comes in but very little daylight. The electric light doesn't work. Cables loop up from the one power point to provide a light. On a hanging lead. That wiring to the power point is old and perished. The kitchen lighting also depends on a cable from the one power point there. In this room the windows don't shut, whatever the weather. But it's dark here too, because the yard is very narrow and light is blocked by the buildings behind. The toilet is in the backyard. The door from the passage to the backyard has no catch and bangs in the wind.[46]

These problems were not confined to private rented dwellings either. In Tower Hamlets in the 1970s the Greater London Council owned and managed some 31,000 homes, and the borough council owned close to 18,000. Their combined role as social landlord came under increasing scrutiny in the 1970s as Bengali families and SHPRS argued that there was distinct and systematic racism in the housing allocation for Bengali families. They argued that the housing waiting list qualification rules were designed to narrow access to Bengali migrant families. Firstly, an applicant to the housing waiting list had to prove five-year residency in the Greater

London Area and fifty-two weeks' continuous residency in Tower Hamlets to even get onto the waiting list. Once they were on the waiting list, a range of institutional and local estate manager racism conspired to make allocations grossly unfair.

After a damning report about the racialised housing discrimination in Hackney in 1984, Dr Deborah Phillips was commissioned by the GLC to conduct an independent audit of housing allocation in Tower Hamlets. Her historical review of the early 1980s is also an indication of some of the deep-seated problems that were faced by Bengali migrants in the 1970s. She identified that the way the system categorised applicants by priority and then insisted on a 'matching process' worked against Bengali migrants, for whom the rigidity of measures required to find a 'match' to vacant homes meant they were less likely to be offered accommodation.[47]

Phillips also recorded that the system allowed ample room for subjective judgements in the grading of applicants and the grading of homes. These gradings had to align for an offer to be made, and Phillips found that this grading system operated against Bengali families. Finally, a systematic review of offers found that Bengali families were more likely to receive a narrower and inferior range of offers based often on what housing officers assumed a Bengali or white family might accept or reject. In addition to this, many Bengali families were keen to stay in the Spitalfields area, having found themselves victims to racist harassment and violence when they were housed in all-white estates. The petition below gives a sense of why Bengali families felt the need to cluster together.

A petition in the following terms has been received from 33 tenants out of the 73 tenants on the Digby Estate:

We the families are rather disturbed about the Asian families applying for the empty flats in Digby Estate. There is already enough trouble between the Asians and the Whites, and we don't see why we should have to put up with anymore. We have our families to think of: and here is our Petition about it:

From Tenants of Digby Estate.

If you are making it into problem flats then you should offer the tenants of Digby Estate other flats to live in. We, the tenants would like to make it plain that we do not want any more Asians on the Digby Estate.

There has been more than enough trouble between the Asians and the White families. There has been gang fights with knives and choppers and we are afraid for our children and the women on the Estate.

It is not good enough when a White girl aged 14 years cannot go up to her flat without an Asian boy stopping her for a kiss on the stairs. Our children are afraid of the Asians. We have had to call our caretaker, Mr. A. Dunn out many times because of the trouble between the Asians and the Whites.

All we want to do is to live in peace on the Estate with our own kind and colour and for our children to have a safe play place to play in.

Thank you.[48]

This petition was at the moderate end of the kind of protests Bengali families encountered – others were far more visceral and violent in their complaints. The demand to be 'able to live in peace ... with our own kind' signals the way the Bengali community were rendered 'alien' and incapable of settling into the white community. The other problem, which was also well documented, was that white council and estate officers often came under direct pressure or were indeed sympathetic to these concerns from white tenants, and would support the victimisation of those Asian families that found themselves isolated in hostile white estates.

At the same time, a burgeoning squatters' movement was emerging in East London, prompted in part by a widespread housing shortage in the post-war period. Don Watson estimates that there were tens of thousands of homeless people and many more living in overcrowded and dilapidated conditions. He notes that this was not simply about shortages but was intimately tied to the growing disconnect that was emerging as a result of slum clearance programmes. While they were, on the one hand, generating better quality housing, these programmes were often inattentive to working-class wage levels, which did not enable families to rent better quality housing.[49]

In 1969 the London Families Squatting Association (LFSA) ran a carefully managed campaign in Redbridge, London, where they identified families on housing waiting lists or languishing in inadequate hostel accommodation and 'opened up' vacant council properties for them to squat. The violence used by the council to evict and prevent further occupation was widely publicised and proved counter-productive, as it generated widespread public sympathy. Rowan Milligan talks about the 'politics of the crowbar' in relation to the squatters' movements that emerged in London between 1968 and 1977. She highlights the number of empty homes – properties that had been decanted ahead of planned redevelopment but then left vacant – versus the staggering housing waiting lists that existed at the same time. Milligan highlights that 'people squatted for many reasons' and that while some used squats as a 'base for political groups and projects', others did so in order to achieve 'affordable housing'; however, she does not create a hierarchy between the motivations for squatting: 'no matter whether you are squatting for a roof over your head or to produce insurrectionary literature in your basement, squatting ought to be seen as a political engagement, the diversity of its aims and make-up only reinforcing the fundamentally radical nature of occupation in itself'.[50]

There are important examples of explicitly political squats in the 1970s. Christine Wall writes about 'sisterhood and squatting' in 1970s Hackney; she explores the experiences of women-only squats, which experimented with alternative models of collective living outside of the heteronormative nuclear family, and which sought to live outside of patriarchal power relations.[51] Matt Cook's research explores the experience and legacy of a gay squatting community in Brixton, South London. His interviewees review their memories through a prism that is inflected with the lives lived beyond their squatting experience. Squatters talked about experimenting with a 'new way of being' and reinventing 'family and home beyond a capitalist framework'.[52]

Cook registers 'cordial relations' between the gay squatter community and the local Black community, some of whom were also squatters.[53] 121 Railton Road was one of those squats and was the site of protracted conflict and police harassment. Olive Morris and Liz Turnbull (Obi) were Black feminist activists and members of the British Black Panthers who squatted 121 Railton Road – a privately owned, empty corner building – at the end of 1972. The premises were secured initially as a home for themselves, but the legal norms of squatting in private property combined with aggressive, racist policing made them subject to particularly vicious attack. The police evictions of the property were forceful and well documented; the famous photograph of Olive Morris climbing back into her squat after such an eviction made the front page of the Advisory Service for Squatters' Handbook in 1979. There was also wider Black squatter activity in and around the area. Obi recalled that there were thin lines of communication across the various squatting communities in and around Railton Road and though there was some intersectional conversation generated by a few Black and gay squatters, on the whole distinct squatter communities were committed to working within their own specific challenges.[54] Olive and Obi eventually relocated their squat to a little further down the road, into a council property that had different legislative norms for eviction.

Railton Road did find a connection to the Bengali squatters over the river in Tower Hamlets. 167 Railton Road later became the base of the *Race Today* collective, which had a vision of Black working-class campaigning that included support for Bengali families in Spitalfields. *Race Today* was critical to the Bengali squatters' movement that developed in Tower Hamlets and the idea of a united 'black' working class. *Race Today* championed the idea of political blackness, which gained a wide consensus in the anti-racist organising of the 1970s and 1980s. This idea was based on the 'rejection of ethnic nationalism' and 'sought to unite all people of colour who had been exploited by colonialism, and oppressed by racism and capitalism'.[55] The idea of political blackness was also embraced by many of the Bengali activists who became involved in the anti-racist activism of the 1970s both inside and outside of the squatter movement.

This political moment arrived just as Britain was coming to terms with the decline of Empire, and the narrative of British national identity was being rewritten in a way that obscured the wealth and resources extracted from the Commonwealth. The roots/routes that had for centuries criss-crossed between Britain and then-nascent Bangladesh were cut off, while legislative attacks stripped away the rights of entry and residence. But Bengali squatters in Spitalfields, whether in Shah Jalol Café or in the sweatshops along Brick Lane, did not see themselves as stealing social resources. On the contrary, there was a sense of accrued belonging and homemaking. The roots/routes of their relationship to Spitalfields were neither accidental nor new.

NOTES

1   Paul Gilroy, *The Black Atlantic: Modernity and Double Consciousness*, Harvard University Press: Cambridge Massachusetts, 1993.

2   Ashfaque Hossain, 'The World of the Sylheti Seamen in the Age of Empire, from the Late Eighteenth Century to 1947', *Journal of Global History*, Vol. 9 (3), 2014, pp425-446.

3   Alexander Crawford Lindsay, *Lives of the Lindsays; or a Memoir of the Houses of Crawford and Balcarres ... To Which Are Added, Extracts from the Official Correspondence of Alex., Sixth Earl of Balcarres, during the Maroon War; Together with Personal Narratives by His Brothers, the Hon. Robert, Colin, James, John, and Hugh Lindsay,* J. Murray: London, 1840, p17.

4   Ibid.

5   Ibid, p28.

6   Ibid, p41.

7   Hossain, op cit, p430.

8   Lindsay, op cit, p108.

9   Caroline Adams, *Across Seven Seas and Thirteen Rivers: Life Stories of Pioneer Sylhetti Settlers in Britain*, THAP: London, 1987.

10 Rozina Visram, *Asians in Britain: Four Hundred Years of History*, Pluto Press: London, 2002.

11 Ibid, p256.

12 Adams, op cit, p187.

13 Hossain, op cit, pp425-446.

14 Lindsay, op. cit., pp85-6.

15 Hossain, op cit, p431.

16 Katy Gardner, Global Migrants, *Local Lives: Travel and Transformation in Rural Bangladesh*, Oxford University Press: Oxford, 1995, p38.

17 Hossain, op cit, p433.
18 Gopal Balachandran, *Globalizing Labour? Indian Seafarers and World Shipping, c. 1879–1945*, Oxford University Press: New Delhi, 2012, p4.
19 Visram, op cit, pp15-16.
20 Ibid, p15.
21 Adams, op cit, p22.
22 Ibid.
23 Heloise Finch-Boyer, 'Lascars through the colonial lens: Reconsidering visual sources of South Asian sailors from the twentieth century' in *Journal for Maritime Research*, 16(2), 2014, p257.
24 Ibid.
25 Balachandran, op cit, p94.
26 Finch-Boyer, op cit, pp260-62.
27 Aaron Jaffer, *Lascars and Indian Ocean Seafaring, 1780-1860: Shipboard Life, Unrest and Mutiny*, Boydell & Brewer, 2015, pp41-42.
28 Visram, op cit, pp256-257.
29 Georgie Wemyss, 'British Indian Seafarers, Bordering and Belonging' in *Routledge Handbook of Critical Studies in Whiteness*, Routledge, 2021, p250.
30 Ibid, p251.
31 Adams, op cit, pp17-18.
32 Ibid, p18.
33 Ibid.
34 Letter from Shipping Federation Ltd, January 1932, National Archives.
35 Ibid.
36 The National Archives: HO 45/14874.
37 Ibid.
38 Wemyss, op cit, p252.
39 Adams, op cit, p37.
40 Sarah Glynn, *Class, Ethnicity and Religion in the Bengali East End: A Political History*, Manchester University Press: Manchester, 2017, p38.
41 Katy Gardner, 'Lives in Motion: The life-course, movement and migration in Bangladesh', *Journal of South Asian Development*, 4(2), 2009, p235.
42 Daniel Willliam Wentworth, *Racial Discrimination in England: Based on the PEP Report*, Penguin Books: Great Britain, 1968.
43 Runnymede Trust, 'Race and Council Housing in London', The Runnymede Trust, 1975.
44 Charlie Forman, *Spitalfields: A Battle for Land*, Hilary Shipman: London, 1989, p30.

45 Ibid, p56.
46 Ibid.
47 Deborah Phillips, 'What price equality? A report on the allocation of GLC housing in Tower Hamlets', Greater London Council, 1986.
48 Tower Hamlets Health and Housing Management Committee minutes, March 1983.
49 Don Watson, *Squatting in Britain 1945-1955: Housing, Politics and Direct Action*, Merlin Press: London, 2016.
50 Rowan T. Milligan, 'The Politics of the Crowbar: Squatting in London, 1968–1977', *Anarchist Studies*, Vol. 24, 2016, p9.
51 Christine Wall, 'Sisterhood and Squatting in the 1970s: Feminism, housing and urban change in Hackney', *History Workshop Journal*, Vol. 83, 2017, pp79-97.
52 Matt Cook, '"Gay times": Identity, locality, memory, and the Brixton squats in 1970's London', *Twentieth Century British History*, Vol. 24, 2013, pp84-109.
53 Ibid, p97.
54 https://rememberolivemorris.wordpress.com.
55 Paul Field, Robin Bunce, Leila Hassan, Margaret Peacock (eds), *Here to Stay, Here to Fight: A Race Today Anthology*, Pluto Press: London, 2019, pp4-5.

2

Claiming home

I can't remember whether it was me or someone else in my family that opened the front door the first time it happened. There was a knock at the door, but no one was there. Within seconds, the knocker sounded again. It was a brass knocker, the kind you have to lift up to rap on the door. Again, we opened the door and were puzzled that no one was there. I think it may have taken three times for this to happen before we realised that a group of white boys had tied fish-wire to the knocker and were hidden behind a wall a few metres away, rolling around in fits of laughter. I can't say for sure if they called out 'Paki' that first time or whether it was on one of the many other occasions, but it soon became clear that this was not just a juvenile prank or joke – it was targeted racism designed to harass us in our new home.

This was late 1980s Hackney. I was eleven years old and we had just moved from the south London estate where I had spent most of my early life, after my parents secured a council tenancy in 1979. Avondale Estate was a mainly white, Corporation of London housing estate, and our presence in a small, ground-floor flat had not been particularly welcomed. We were frozen out of estate networks, and our childhood play in the central concrete square was littered with racist insults and even occasional violence. But more routinely, we were simply but firmly made to feel that we were both inferior and unwanted.

In our new house in Hackney, our parents had promised a more mixed area and reprieve from the racist isolation that we had grown up with. But our front door was often the site of racist harassment, whether it was the occasional egg throwing, kicks to the door, or the more traditional (racially tinted) version of 'knock-down-ginger'. By this time, my father had gone from working full-time as a kitchen porter and working in his spare time alongside my mum as a home-garments worker, to now co-owning a restaurant in Exmouth Market in partnership with an uncle. The area was up-and-coming and business was good. Fay Maschler, a famous Evening Standard restaurant critic, came and gave the restaurant – and my dad's cooking – rave reviews, for the quality of curries she ate and the warm service she received. That review was framed and took pride of place in the front window of the restaurant. Like other 'Indian' restaurants of the time, the menu was modified to cater for the British palate, and the burgundy flocked wallpaper, along with the pile of poppadoms and the metal table-top carousel of sweet and sour pickles, became a regular haunt for locals on a Friday night.

Not so regular, but often enough, were the occasions when bricks and rocks were thrown through the big front window; when after consuming a meal and enjoying the hospitality of the service, customers refused to pay their bill and instead trashed the restaurant, throwing a chair to smash the window as they left. Even at a young age, I was aware that our homes and businesses were precarious spaces, that there were margins here between 'us' and 'them' where the outside world would make known that no matter how much we tried to fit in, we were unwelcome. In many ways, those thresholds of doors and windows and the interactions that happen there have long marked migrant experiences of settlement and homemaking, including for Bengali squatters.

'I SAID, "WE NEED TO GET IN THERE". SO I ... I WENT AND I BROKE THE DOOR'

Abdul Kadir arrived in London in 1957. He was following in his father's footsteps, a man who had worked on English ships for decades before Kadir's arrival. After experiencing severe housing difficulties and having petitioned the council for housing, Kadir and his wife Sufia ended up squatting their first few family houses

Abdul Kadir © Kois Miah 2020.

in Spitalfields before eventually securing tenancy rights by the late 1970s. They spent decades remitting to an extended family that remained in Sylhet and built a remittance house in Sylhet town. Now retired, they rely on a close family network of children and grandchildren and continue to live in East London.

Like most single Bengali men, Kadir had started life in East London staying in different multiple-occupancy properties before he applied for his family to join him. The initial decision to apply was motivated by a health emergency and the family had no intention of staying. However, life events meant that the family stayed on. They started out in a small, one-bedroom flat near Brick Lane while the regular tenant was visiting Bangladesh. However, the space was too small for a family of five and Sufia was pregnant. Kadir had applied for a council flat well before their arrival and he went back repeatedly, informing them of his more urgent need for accommodation. He described the indifference that his appeals were met with and the way that housing officers would shirk their responsibility for his family's housing need. Finally, Kadir decided to take matters into his own hands:

> And that's when it was being said that lots of people were squatting. There was a man called Terry in this area, I asked him and he said, 'I can get you in a building', he got lots of our people in. Terry said, 'Greenleaf House'.[1] I'm emptying a building', I think there was a one-room, two-room flat, on the second floor in Greenleaf House. We went, but even there it wasn't adequate. He changed the locks and changed the door, and we went in with all our stuff, and then the police came. They came quickly, the police said, 'You've entered here – you know this is council property and you shouldn't be here'. I said – and I know how to speak English by this time – I said, 'I know this is a council flat, but I haven't got anywhere to go and this is empty'. They said, 'You can't stay'. I said, 'Well, when I can't, I can't, but where else have I got to stay?' And in that quick time, with so much speed, I had already thrown a couple of mattresses on the floor. The police argued with me, they said 'You can't stay here, it's against the law, you have to get out', and I just said, 'Where else can I go?'

When asked about whether he was worried by the interaction, he stated defiantly that he had no choice but to stand his ground; his housing situation was so dire that whatever anxieties he had about disobeying the police officers were diminished by the needs of his young family. The man that had helped Kadir to find and obtain the squat was Terry Fitzpatrick, someone who was familiar to all the Bengali squatters that I interviewed, either directly or indirectly. His role in the Bengali squatters' movement was critical, and for many like Kadir he was their entry point to squatting in terms of giving both advice and practical support for breaking in and occupying a property.

Terry's relationship with the Bengali community is explored later, but for Kadir and his family the first squat that Terry helped to open up was in such poor condition that the family had to go back to renting privately while they waited on the council for an offer of housing again. As explored earlier, the way that the housing allocation system operated created an opportunity for individual housing officers to exercise discretion in how and to whom they offered vacant properties, while at the same time guidance on matching applicants to properties meant that vacant properties were routinely identified as a poor match for Bengali families. Deborah Phillips' report 'What price equality: A report on the allocation of GLC housing in Tower Hamlets' also concluded that the allocation system gave considerable discretion to housing officers, who were able to judge an applicants' 'worth' and what they might deserve.[2] Kadir's family returned to renting, but as described by Charlie Forman, many of the tenement buildings that offered cheap private rent were in terrible condition: '[w]hat had been considered unfit for the working class of nineteenth-century London was being lived in a century later with a hundred years of disrepair to add to the misery'.[3]

Kadir described the flat that they managed to rent near Petticoat Lane Market in Spitalfields. Located on the fourth floor of the building, it had no bath – which was not uncommon – and had a cooker that was plugged in at the back of the flat on the outside balcony. He remembers that their downstairs neighbour was a disagreeable man who would regularly arrive at their front door complaining about the noise of his young children. After some months of paying rent for what was essentially an uninhabitable property, Kadir recalls spotting a newly vacated flat on a nearby council estate:

> I saw the flat we went into, that flat was empty, there had been some white people there but they had just left. I said to her [indicates his wife, Sufia], 'I want to occupy that flat', but I said, 'Will you be able to stay there? There are lots of white people – lots of the bad kind ... all around.' She said, 'Whatever will happen, will happen, we need to live'. I said, 'Well then, we need to get in there quickly'. So I went and I broke the door ... I broke the door, and once inside I called out to someone I knew, I got him to stay there. You needed to have a mattress or two to claim it, so all the way from my flat, I got a mattress, I carried it all the way over ... So, I got

it in and then got her [indicates Sufia] to come quickly and sit down. And that's when we were pelted with stones, from all directions. Stones everywhere, those boys – there was a play area just nearby, there was a netted area, they all started throwing stones, they broke all the glass, the front and side window all of them.

Kadir and his wife Sufia described the terror of this moment. They had only just managed to enter and occupy the property and Kadir was still breathless from the strain of carrying the mattresses. It was in the first quiet moments of having entered and shut the front door that the onslaught started. The estate was almost wholly made up of white tenants and Kadir and Sufia's act of occupation had not gone unnoticed. It was not unexpected, but the swiftness of the reaction nevertheless caught them off guard. Within minutes and accompanied by a barrage of racist abuse, rocks and stones smashed through every glass panel in the front of house. Kadir responded by grabbing a *dha* (a floor-based kitchen knife common in South Asia) and raced outside to confront the boys – who all laughed and shouted as they ran away.

So I had to clean it all up again, and then did what I could with the mattresses and things we had brought over. Then the police came … The police came, not to see who had broken the windows – but to ask why we were there and for us to get out. And we said, 'Where would we go?' I said, 'We applied two years ago, they don't give us a flat or anything else, where do you want us to go? If you need to take us to court, do it! Go away!' I said that! After that came the estate officer, he was such a bad estate officer, he came and said go away and said dirty things to us. I said, 'Don't speak to me in a dirty way or I'll chop you!' He carried on saying 'get out of here', I said, 'You take me to court or give me a rent book!'

Kadir was adamant that he was *entitled* to council housing and despite a long campaign to obtain a tenancy he says that, like most other Bengali families struggling in overcrowded conditions, he was never made a single housing offer. He was not looking to avoid paying rent, quite the opposite; he hoped that squatting might force the council to award him a tenancy. He 'claimed' the flat by what was colloquially accepted as the marker of squatted occupation: hastily retrieving a mattress and throwing it down. In a documentary series produced by local filmmaker and photographer, Simon Heaven, who was based at the local Montefiore Community Centre at the time, Kadir features in a housing action meeting of about twenty Bengali men, where he challenges the council's disregard for his young family's hardship:

> I am waiting for the last five years for Tower Hamlets, Tower Hamlet council. They ... didn't give me any flat. So what I have to do? I get only one room. We are living six, seven people. Seven members of us, no bath, no proper toilets and I couldn't get any other flat. I can't buy any flat myself because there is no house for selling in this area. So, where do I have to live?! We have to be squatting. We can't stay on the street with a little kid. We are – therefore Bengali people, we have to do these things.

Abdul Kadir in *A Safe Place to Be*, by Simon Heaven.
Compass Films, 1980 (BFI archives).

Kadir's frustration was rooted in an understanding which surfaced repeatedly in his interview: that he had 'long family links', he was a 'legal citizen', a 'long-term worker', 'a taxpayer' and 'resident of the local community'. All of this was denied by the council, who treated him and other Bengali families as unwelcome 'new' arrivals, a narrative premised on popularised 1970s colonial amnesia. This state discrimination was matched by the white neighbours, who had responded with the hail of bricks and stones that shattered every glass panel in the front of house space, and then by the repeated threats of the estate manager.

This hostility at the front of their house would have been entirely at odds with their home experiences in rural Sylhet. The *bari*, or rural dwelling, that both Kadir and Sufia had experienced was organised around a concentric zonal system, which regulated who was permitted to approach the dwelling. The family's privacy and security were guarded not by the convention of glass windows and front doors, but by implicit social rules about familiarity and proximity of family relations. Windows, on the other hand, have a different liminal, or in-between, quality, where those on the inside generally have the capacity, through their soft furnishings, to select where the 'public space of "outside" is supposed to finish and the private space of the home start'.[4] Even so, there is more fragility in that threshold space. In the case of Kadir and Sufia, and many hundreds of other Bengali migrants, the racialised expectations of who 'belonged' to the neighbourhood were often violently played out in those door and window spaces. The breaking of windows meant that the racial hostility of the street outside crashed into the space they had claimed just moments earlier, immediately rendering it a space of vulnerability and threat. Kadir's response was to take up a *dha* and to emerge from the flat to threaten the boys, who in this instance quickly dispersed, but who remained regular perpetrators of violence and intimidation, calling his children 'Pakis' and telling them to 'go back home'.

This racialised 'un-homing' violence was littered throughout archival sources and included letters of complaint to local newspapers and tenant petitions organised by whole estates stating that Bengali migrants were unwelcome and alien to the East End:

It has taken the British people many years to evolve our present culture where it is generally regarded that one family per house is quite sufficient, then along come the immigrants to whom three, four and five families is nothing unusual. They then turn what were recently quiet respectable streets into overcrowded slums.

Am I a racialist? Well if a racialist is someone who is sick and tired of seeing British people living in hostels for the homeless and the immigrants flooding in, then I am a racialist.

If a racialist is someone who is fed up with being told that our schools and classrooms are overcrowded and then sees the playgrounds full of immigrant children then I am a racialist.

It would do our politicians well to remember that you can only sweep a certain amount of dirt under the carpet before someone falls over the lump. The lump is now swelling ominously.[5]

The letter illustrates the popular narrative that the Bengali community had usurped the rightful 'British people' of their housing rights and needs. In fact, the reaction to Kadir and Sufia may not have been different had they been formally offered the property by the council – many Bengali families recalled a similar reception even when they had moved in with official tenancy agreements. It is also interesting to note that Bengali families were dismissed as having a primitive culture and that the overcrowding they experienced was seen as a matter of *choice*, even a cultural norm, rather than a feature of the housing crisis they suffered. This assumption sits in sharp contrast to the expansive home space most of the Bengali families had enjoyed in rural Sylhet. The hostility of the letter echoes the rocks and stones that crashed through the windows of Kadir and Sufia's squatted home. It expresses anger that the social provisions to which the white British community felt entitled were being depleted by this 'undeserving' group of migrants and contradicts Kadir's claim that he and his family had an accrued investment and therefore a right to these social resources. Kadir was one of the first to squat on that estate, but soon after other Bengali families joined, and he offered support and solidarity to others that came and experienced something of that hostility. He was also critical in helping these Bengali families to seek and obtain legal advice and became an active organiser for the group of squatters that came to occupy flats in that same building and beyond.

Sufia (pictured below), Abdul Kadir's wife, had settled in London as a reluctant migrant. Her grandfather, father and uncles had variously worked on English ships and lived in East London long before her birth, but she stressed that she herself had never aspired to being a *Londoni*. At the time I interviewed her she was around seventy-three years of age, in good health and, like her husband, lively in her words. She recalled that she was regularly at home alone with her children while Kadir worked in a garment factory on Brick Lane. He worked long hours and she remembers the council worker that Kadir referred to regularly banging on her front door: he would 'come and give me trouble and he would threaten me and I would just threaten him back – he was a bad sort'.

Sufia Begum © Kois Miah 2020.

Sufia talked at length about the hardships she faced. She was, by then, a mother of four young children, and occasionally undertook piece work on a sewing machine at home. She also saw herself as the defender of their squatted home and stated pragmatically that 'whatever you are dealt – you have to work with it'. She acknowledged that others would have found the visits by the local estate officer frightening, but like her husband, she shrugged: 'I was courageous, I said, 'I won't leave!' I wasn't scared – how are you going to live if you aren't courageous? They weren't giving it to you!'

This articulation of claiming and appropriating something that she felt she was otherwise owed, and her defiance in those conversations with the estate manager, was echoed by other Bengali women in her position. It was one of the informal squatter rules that leaving the squat unguarded could result in a council official breaking in and 'reclaiming' the flat so many Bengali women, at least in the early days of establishing their squat, were obliged to remain at home to assert the claim to home. Nothing in the documentary and media archives hints at these female Bengali voices of opposition. The Bengali women that appear in photographs of the 1970s and in the BFI film archives appear fleetingly as vulnerable and muted characters that are peripheral to the main story. However, the realities of the squatted home and the nature of gendered labour patterns (Bengali women often working from home) meant that women were effectively the day-to-day guardians of the squat and were the ones most likely to experience and navigate the state and street violence that encircled those spaces.

Shafia, another female squatter, is now in her late sixties. She married her older sister's husband when her sister unexpectedly passed away, becoming step-mother to her nephew and nieces. Her husband was older, and she recalls the misery of living in badly overcrowded accommodation with the young children. When she heard from others around her that Bengali families were squatting, she began to counsel her husband to do the same. She even recalled agreeing with a female neighbour, also desperate to escape her crowded living conditions, to approach Terry Fitzpatrick to help them obtain a squat without their husbands' consent. In the event, her husband initiated the conversation and the family squatted an empty property on Varden Street. Here, Shafia recalls, 'I had a lot of courage, I wasn't scared'. Like Sufia, Shafia engaged in defiant conversations whenever she was visited by council officials, who intermittently came round to demand that they vacate the property. She recalls clearly standing by the front door, engaging in conversations that she laughingly says she barely understood:

> What they were saying, who knows? But you can tell from their tone, can't you? But I said whatever I could. I would just say, 'Come back another day – I don't understand'. I did understand – of course I understand, they were telling me to get out, but I just kept saying I didn't understand! [laughs]

Mashuk Miah arrived in London in 1973 as a fifteen-year-old boy with his mother and two brothers. The family initially stayed with his *sasa*'s (paternal uncle) family in Weaver House; the two families, comprising ten people, were squeezed into a three-bedroom flat. He recollects that his father, who had been in the UK for over a decade by this point, had made efforts to apply for council housing only to be told that without a fifty-two-week proof of continuous residency in Tower Hamlets, he was not eligible to be on the council waiting list. His father's previous decade-long stay was disqualified because he had, like many other migrant men, made a short trip home to accompany his family when they migrated. His father then made a strategic decision, one that was designed to navigate their way onto the housing list: squatting.

> My dad hadn't stayed here. It was the law at the time, you had to stay here for fifty-two weeks, and you have to provide your proof and only then we're gonna take you, after that. In between, we – that's when we went to the squat. Some people suggested it to us. That's how people were staying, from Desh, they were staying like that so that they got their fifty-two weeks proof *and* they had somewhere to stay. If there was an empty house they would get the furniture and stay there.

The five-year Greater London residency qualification, the fifty-two-week continuous residence policy in Tower Hamlets, and the significant discretion given to individual housing officers all conspired to create a discriminatory allocation system. They specifically impacted the ability for Bengali migrant families, who may well have had at least one member residing in the borough for many decades, to obtain the housing to which they felt they were entitled. Mashuk's father, with the support of sympathetic white squatters, went along to a flat he had spotted in the same building where he was sharing a flat with his brother's family. They broke in, changed the locks and claimed the space by moving in some beds. Mashuk says that he recalls the family getting an eviction notice early on: 'They said we have to get out and they would get us out – but we said, "Where can we go?" And we said, "But we are a family, we're not single – where can we go?"'

Apart from this early interaction, Mashuk says that the family were basically left alone; they lived there 'like it was our own house'. He gathered that this was because the council simply did not have the resources to deal with the sudden increase in squatting. The family managed to squat this flat for two years; however, they were still determined to secure a permanent tenancy, and Mashuk explained the decision to squat as being, in part, for the family to fulfil the requirements for council housing. His father applied for housing once they had been in their squat for fifty-two weeks and reached the qualifying residency threshold. After a further year, they accepted the council's offer to 'go homeless', which meant they were placed in temporary accommodation in a hotel in Finsbury Park before being rehoused to a flat in Bethnal Green.

Unlike the squat, which the family found and appropriated on their terms, the council flat they were eventually allocated moved them out of the Spitalfields area and onto the border near Bethnal Green, a short distance away, but with significant security implications:

When we got a flat, after we went homeless, the flat we got – it was in Bethnal Green, Hollybush House, Hollybush Street. That area – the National Front, that was where they had their main office … so we had got a flat having gone homeless, it looked okay, and there was a few Afro-Caribbean people and so we got along with them. We stayed a few days – and then it turned out that the National Front boys would come in the evening and would gather around the building. Every evening, about sixty or seventy – sometimes a hundred boys here – they would gather around the building. Me and my other brother, they wouldn't do anything to us, but if they saw someone older, they would spit on them or they would throw things at them and swear at them and call them Paki ... They didn't do that to us – we were young, we might fight back, that's why. And also, we had a group, we were friends and we used to come and go and there were a few of us and they would see we had friends, so that's why they didn't mess with us, they were our age, these boys ...

One day about 9 o'clock they came – they had come much earlier – and then about nine, ten, the boys started throwing bricks at our window. The glass in the whole place, the whole flat was smashed, every bit of the flat. We were inside. Everything smashed! All smashed. They smashed everything. So me and my two brothers, we wanted to retaliate, but our parents said, 'No! Don't you dare.' My mum and dad, they said don't go out but we did, we were young, seventeen or eighteen, and we threw some things back, but there were nearly seventy of them so it did nothing and our parents were saying, 'No, don't go out'.

We stayed there that night. We called the police, the police came. At that time not everyone had a phone, our next door – the African people, they called the police, once the boys were throwing. The police came, but the police came with their sirens on and so of course all the boys ran away, so no one was there, just us, the victims, in the house, so they said, 'Do you know them, do you recognise them?' How could we? There about 100 of them, and they don't live in this building, these boys, they're from the outside, just roaming this area.

The next day we left. We went to another building, we found an empty flat, there were people leaving that flat and we went inside. So we were back to squatting again. We stayed there a few days. But this time they didn't let us stay there like before because the family that had just left, they were going homeless and they had been squatters too, and they hadn't told us they were being evicted, and that evening we went in. And the next, next day when the workmen came around to clean, they found us people already in there [laughs]. They said, 'You have to get out, we won't accept this, we won't accept it, you have to get out!' We said, 'But where do we have we to go? This is what happened to us, ask the police, there's a report'.

Having waited years for a council tenancy, Mashuk's family found themselves the victims of violent and targeted racism. In his account, he is aware that this hostility had a very specific target; their direct neighbours, an African-Caribbean family who were longer-term residents of this estate – who likely had experienced racist abuse earlier in their own residency – were left undisturbed. The contrasting treatment of the two families hints at the complexity of racism in 1970s London. Mashuk's account reveals the specific ways in which colonial constructions of race in this instance marked out the Bengali community as the unwelcome Other. In Mashuk's case this was experienced as a violent un-homing encounter in his family's newly acquired council home.

In a 1978 episode of *Credo*, a London Weekend Television (LWT) religious affairs series, the opening credits show a window being smashed. The next frame shows a Bengali family – two adults and two children – sat on a bed in front of a large window, with what looks like an olive-green bed sheet covering it. The Bengali woman, though included in the initial shot, is then cut out of view as the man explains through a Bengali interpreter that their windows were regularly broken by racist neighbours, who would 'throw bricks, bottle, whatever they can get hold of …' and kick down their front door.

Credo, LWT 1978 (BFI Archives).

The narrator of the documentary observed that 'the Bengalis have often seemed far easier targets than other immigrant groups and have been the victim of much greater number of attacks than for example the West Indians in the same area'. The main Bengali interviewee, Gulam Mustafa, Secretary of Brick Lane Jamme Masjid, agreed that this was because Bengali Muslims were a 'passive' and 'peace-loving people'. There follow several other interviews where the discussion is about the 'little Bengali tailor' and specifically their cultural temperament that supposedly makes them vulnerable to attack:

> It's basically the Sylhetis that are copping the brunt of the violence and harassment. They speak little English, they come from a totally different – rural to urban, city … they are people unused to the way of life here, they have a tradition of being very peaceful people, of very non-violent people. In a strange way, the expectation of the lads on the street here, the local kids, is for the men, the boy, to show his manhood by fighting back – by hitting. There's a kind of urge from the host community for people to fight back. People say they respect the West Indian lads because they can fight – can look after themselves. There's a kind of urge to violence that's kind of expected of the Bengali community by the host community in a strange way.[6]

The views expressed here suggest that 'belonging' was not simply contingent on being white. Mashuk's family were un-homed by the specific way that the Bengali community was targeted – their windows were shattered, but not the windows of their Black neighbours. The West Indian community, who the Bengali community were compared to in the documentary, certainly did not escape racism – the post-war migration era saw decades of bloody and brutal racist violence and discrimination against them – but at times young Black men were able to operate within racially mixed friendship groups in a way that was impossible for their Bengali equivalents, at least in the 1970s.

This dynamic is well illustrated in Susie Daniel and Pete McGuire's *The Paint House: Words from an East End Gang*. In this 'insider' account of the East End Collinwood Gang, the group of mainly white English, but also West Indian, young men talk glee-fully about their 'Paki-bashing sprees'.[7] This speaks to the pernicious way in which racism divides communities into different groups and subjects them to specific systems of exclusion, co-opting certain communities at historical moments, often in complex and contra-dictory ways. The idea of some West Indian young men being perpetrators of violence against Bengali youth would seem contra-dictory given the violence their communities also experienced. This points to the 'organic' character of racism, producing insiders and outsiders, marking out those who 'belong' at a given point in time from those who do not, in ways that evoke 'common-sense' notions about racialised groups. For example, while West Indian young men were pathologised as aggressive and violent, Bengalis were characterised as physically weak and passive and therefore blamed for the racist violence that they experienced.

These ideas about the 'passive Bengali' reach back to the racial-ised tropes of the Indian lascars discussed in the previous chapter and are rooted in a longer arc of colonial experience. Paul Dimeo describes the constructs of 'martial' Punjabis and 'effeminate' Bengalis as part of a wider strategy used by the British to secure power in India. In the Indian Rebellion of 1857, Punjabis had remained 'loyal' to the British forces while Bengalis had been at the forefront of the uprising. Dimeo argues that this coincided with an essentialist and fixed view of 'race' that became prevalent in the mid nineteenth century in the West. Bengalis were viewed with suspicion and male Bengali bodies were 'looked down upon with disgust and contempt'.[8] Dimeo's work explores how sport in colo-nial India was used to support this ideology of racial hierarchy

> to morally justify colonial rule as a benevolent gesture towards people supposedly lacking either the physical strength, will-power, intelligence and resourcefulness to run their own country. The strong body 'as metaphor for security' was only available to European men; non-Europeans and women were treated like children who required protection and guidance. Improvements could only be made through the methods imposed, controlled and defined by the male colonial rulers.[9]

The construct of Bengali men as effeminate that originated as a method of control in colonial India was translated into the caricature of Bengali people as passive and alien to the 'street tough' culture of the East End.

The complex racialised and gendered tapestry evident in the street violence was also intersected by generational differences. Mashuk recognised that he and his brother were less likely victims of direct street-based racist violence, pointing out that 'if they saw someone older – they would spit on them or they would throw things at them and swear at them and call them Paki ... Not to us ... We were young, we might fight back'. The racist violence in the window space instigated terror in the moment but also highlighted a moment of tension and conflict between the two generations inside. His parents forbade him and his brother from leaving the safer – though breached – inside space of the home, but Mashuk and his young brother refused to listen and emerged to throw a few token bricks back. This generational divergence on how best to navigate racist attacks is revisited in Chapters Three and Four and highlights how the caricature of effeminacy was contradicted by patterns of resistance on the ground. For Mashuk and his family, the insecurity generated in their front of house space in this incident meant that, having secured this tenancy after years of squatting, the family were effectively un-homed, and they returned to squatting as their escape. Squatting was therefore a way to obtain housing in desperate conditions, often as a result of how institutional and street racism interacted to leave Bengali families isolated on notoriously racist estates.

Soyful was eighteen years old when he arrived in the UK to join his father in 1977. His father had been in London since 1965 and worked as a machinist. Soyful had barely known him as a child except for the infrequent, recuperative holidays his father took to Bangladesh. Once in London, that pattern changed little:

> He used to work in tailoring and he used to work very long hours. I think many Bengalis that came here, they used to work very long hours. They used to go to workshop at six o'clock in the morning, finish about eight, nine, ten o'clock. They never saw the daylight because of their working life, they never used

to see daylight, so that's how it was for them. They did the work that no one else was doing and in an environment that no one else would work.

Despite having been in Tower Hamlets some twelve years by the time his family arrived, Soyful's father was unable to secure council accommodation. The family of six arrived to stay in one room and moved around, sometimes splitting up and other times regrouping in the various different accommodations they stayed in over a period of several months. For Soyful, like other Bengali migrants, this was considerably worse than his previous experiences of home. In Bangladesh they had lived in rural Sylhet. His grandfather was a reasonably affluent, land-holding farmer, and his father's remittance income had helped to secure a comfortable life for him and the wider family. That remittance income became part of his responsibility when they arrived in London and despite his ambitions to become a 'medical practitioner', both Soyful and his brother joined his father in tailoring work. It was the hardship of this initial period, the overcrowding and the desperation for some housing security, which drew them to squatting. Observing the widespread nature of squatting in 1978, Soyful and his family squatted first in Nelson Street and then in Parfett Street:

> Everybody was squatting. There was about 100 property in this area so we all squatted and so on, and some people paid key money, some people squatted by force – they just did it themselves, by breaking in. And so we moved into a squatted property in Parfett Street. We paid some money to a *dalal* (intermediary) and took the key money, and we shared a four-storey building – two storey belonged to us and two storey to another family.

Soyful sees these early experiences – along with the understanding of them he achieved through attending evening classes at the Whitechapel Centre, where he met Bengali teachers, intellectuals and other young men – as the grounding for the long activist and political career he went on to have in Tower Hamlets. As an adult, he became a campaigner around housing and education through local community centres and tenants' associations, but later also as a local councillor.

Unlike these families who deliberately squatted, my parents, Abdul Masabbir and Guljahan, were 'accidental' squatters. Along with another couple, they paid a local man who presented himself as a private landlord a sizeable deposit to secure a rent book for 12 Deal Street, a small, dilapidated house just off Brick Lane. They came to realise there was a problem when, after a few days of moving into their house, council officials visited, inquiring how they had come to enter a council-condemned property. This was not uncommon; reports from the time indicate that many were duped by 'imposter' landlords who forged documents and rent books, and extorted money from desperate families who had little experience of the housing system in the UK. The visit from the council was followed by notices to leave. In addition to this, the 'landlord' returned repeatedly with a group of *goondas* (thugs), who would bang on the door demanding 'rent money', which my parents refused to pay. Masabbir explained:

> [...] this man had got a duplicate key and taken our £500 and he used to stay on Roper Street ... and he was making money from us people. But I got in big trouble because I had spent the money on the furniture – I had spent £500 – and on hearing this, the man who had come in with me – I came home from work and found that he had gone to squat on the other side of the road! Taking my beds and blankets, right opposite, eighteen number, eighteen or twenty, I've forgotten. That house is still there. Others had done it, and people had told him that no one can get you out, you won't have to pay £25 rent and you won't have to put up with that man shouting at you. That man made up his mind and he just went. Now I was alone with my wife in that house and also my wife didn't know English, and I didn't want to leave my job. That man kept coming, he would come and demand rent and she was scared that she didn't know any English or what to say. It was really hard.

It is interesting that Masabbir's co-tenant recognised the rogue landlord as a bigger threat to his family's housing security than the council and decided to leave Masabbir – both of them £500 out of pocket – to squat in a property across the road, presumably with the belief that the council was less aggressive in its handling of squatters than the rogue landlord. This decision left Masabbir's wife, eldest daughter Rasna, and new baby (me) alone in the house for much of the time. Again, there is a gendered aspect to this experience in that Masabbir's job as a sous chef in a restaurant in the City meant that he was out of the house for much of the day and early evening, while Guljahan, who had taken on home stitching work and had two young children, was now, like Sufia and Shafia, at home by herself. In his account, Masabbir lamented the lack of council housing offered to 'hardworking, legal migrants' and accepted that he simply did not possess the English literacy skills he needed to petition his case. He did seek support from local advice services, but the persistent threats from the council and 'landlord' were deeply distressing.

At the time Guljahan, my mother, was a twenty-year-old woman. She described how happy she had first been when learning that, after six years of marriage, and having stayed with her in-laws at their village residence, she was leaving to come to London to join her husband:

I was happy, I was really happy! I was going! I wouldn't have to do this work anymore! [laughs] But when I came here, I thought – oh my God! Where have I come? I can't go home to Khujar Khola [her family village] anymore! When I came here, I didn't like it, but when I left [Sylhet], I had been so happy to come – after all those attempts to get entry, everyone was happy, everyone was happy I was coming.

Just before Guljahan left, she took a photograph with her mother-in-law and her first child, Rasna (see below). The standard studio backdrop used for the photograph is a picture of a ship, a nod to the long shipping connection between Sylhet and East London referred to in Chapter One. Neither Guljahan nor Masabbir had direct family that had travelled to London as part of that maritime labour force – they were both first generation international migrants from their respective families – but this photograph highlights that the shipping connection of earlier Bengali seafarers was part of the popular imaginary of the connection between London and Sylhet for Bengali migrants.

Family photograph taken in 1975, before Guljahan
migrated to London.

Georgie Wemyss's scholarship highlights the contrasting popular
imaginary at the other end of that relationship, in the host population in London. She argues that the kind of un-homing violence
described above was justified not only by a sense that the Bengali
community were the unwelcome Other, but also that they were
a *new and illegitimate* community of migrants who were seeking
access to social resources to which they were not entitled:

> The mobile, global labour force of British Indian seafarers was
> central to the economies of the British Empire and to Britain's
> survival in two world wars. However, due to the invisibility
> of their bodies and experiences, produced and enforced by
> imperial, racialised, border legislation and everyday bordering
> practices, their lives have been ignored in dominant white
> narratives of British history and settler colonies.[10]

Gurminder Bhambra has also written extensively about how colonial migrants who came to work in Britain, who saw themselves as part of the British Empire's polity, arrived only to find their rights 'called into question by the local population, who were either unaware of them or indifferent'.[11] Bhambra highlights the power of this sentiment in the popular imaginary, and how these narratives have been endorsed not just in archival letters to newspapers, but also by more recent, 'authoritative' sources. For example, Geoff Dench, Kate Gavron and Michael Young, writing in 'The New East End', reinforce the idea that: '[A]s newcomers, their families cannot have put much into the system, so they should not be expecting yet to take so much out.'[12]

Guljahan may have been a recent migrant, but she was clear that her husband was not. She had, like many young Bengali brides of the time, only known her husband as a transnational commuter for the first six years of their marriage. When interviewed, Guljahan described her excitement at leaving Sylhet, mainly, she says, because she disliked working in her husband's household. The family was a reasonably affluent farming family, and while most of the work was done by labourers, during the harvest season extra work had to be completed quickly and everyone in the family would be called upon to ensure the grain was threshed on time. Ironically, their move to Deal Street in London was partly motivated by the fact that Guljahan would be close enough to the garment factories of Brick Lane and could have piece work delivered to the house. This challenges the trope that Bengali women remained inside the home because of traditional gender roles, and instead highlights that, in many cases, Bengali women – often described as 'family reunification migrants' – were also active economic migrants. In Guljahan's case, even as a mother of two young children, she was earning to send remittances to supplement those earned by her husband.

Having realised that what they thought was a privately rented property was now essentially a squatted house, the couple related the sense of anxiety and stress created by the so-called landlord, who continued to insist they pay rent to him, and the local council, who returned repeatedly with notices to vacate. This insecurity at the front threshold to their house invaded their sense of well-being and deprived them of being able to feel 'at home'. Guljahan recounts how her husband was intimidated by the rogue 'landlord', whose *goondas* would arrive at all times of the day and night, banging loudly on the door and loitering outside the house. On more than one occasion there were violent altercations between Masabbir and the *goondas* that travelled with the 'landlord' as he went around collecting his 'rent'. Part of their discomfort was also *shorom* – the *shame* of the situation: the 'landlord's' threat was that he would break down the door and throw their belongings out onto the street. Guljahan also recounts fearing that the council might eventually involve the police, and that they would do the same.

These encounters not only contradicted the cultural etiquette of the rural Sylheti dwelling, but the loud and hostile attention drawn to them as squatters was something that deprived Masabbir and Guljahan of their sense of security and dignity. Though squatting was not a criminal matter at the time, the couple were unsure of their legal position, and having heard stories where families were physically thrown out of their homes, their possessions strewn on the road, they felt that insisting on staying was not worth the risk. After around nine months of harassment, my parents were effectively un-homed by these experiences and fled the 'accidental' squat. They found a reprieve on the floor of a family relation's rented flat on the other side of London and continued to experience significant housing hardship for three more years.

These experiences of harassment by neighbours and council officials, though deeply traumatic, were at the more moderate end of the violence that some Bengali families experienced. Abdul Mumin's story was highlighted in a *Race Today* article from 1975. He was one of the 'fortunate' families who, after three years of waiting on the council list, was offered a property in Poplar.[13] He described, as did others, that the council official that took them to visit the property was dismissive of the family's concerns when they pointed out that the flat was riddled with damp, that the wallpaper was peeling off the walls and that the stench from the bathroom was unbearable. It was made clear that it was a case of take it or lose out on any further offers. Desperate for accommodation, the family moved in anyway. In the time they spent there, Mumin's infant child died of pneumonia, a death he blamed on the damp.[14] But the awful condition of the flat was not their only concern; Mumin's family were the only Bengali family on the estate and their presence soon attracted unwanted attention. The family were regularly attacked as they made their way around the estate, but the final straw came when the flat was set on fire in an arson attack. After this, Mumin and his family gave up their tenancy and moved back into the familiar surrounds of Spitalfields to squat.

The stories shared here tell us that Bengali families arrived at squatting in a number of different ways. Some squatted out of immediate desperation; others saw it as a strategy through which to fulfil the strict housing waiting list criteria; and others squatted after getting secure tenancies but deciding that the tenancy was not worth their lives, and that the insecurity of squatting was preferable to the regularised and brutal violence that they encountered in isolated flats and houses, away from the Bengali community.

MOVING IN AND OUT AGAIN

Although it started with individual Bengali families breaking into vacant houses dotted around the Spitalfields area, by the mid 1970s squatting had gathered a collective momentum in the community. With the number of families squatting increasing, and through the prominent involvement of white squatter activist Terry Fitzpatrick, the housing issue came to the attention of a group of Black Power activists called the *Race Today* collective, who were based at Railton Road, Brixton.

The *Race Today* collective emerged out of the Institute for Race Relations (IRR). Darcus Howe, nephew of the Trinidadian intellectual C. L. R. James, had risen to prominence partly as a result of self-representing in the 'Mangrove Nine' trial, a case resulting from police harassment of a popular West Indian restaurant. After the conclusion of the case in 1967, Howe went on to join the British Black Panthers and become editor of the IRR's monthly journal, *Race Today*. It was here that he met Farrukh Dhondy and Mala Sen, both of whom were affluent Indian migrants and activists in their own right. Mala's family were from West Bengal in India and she could speak Bengali, which became critical to the collective's ability to later support Bengali squatters. Conflict in leadership and disciplinary style led to a split and the eventual dissolution of the British

Black Panthers. The split saw Howe take the *Race Today* journal, along with Dhondy and Sen, to create a new collective based in Brixton's Railton Road community. Robin Bunce and Paul Field describe this as a 'radical break with the past', suggesting that '[r]ather than proceed on "liberal" assumptions that black people were helpless victims', *Race Today* would reflect the '"self-activity" of the Caribbean and Asian peoples'.[15] What was critical in this political discourse was that the political concept 'Black' was inclusive of Asian people, through an acknowledgement of the synergy between historical and ongoing struggles in former colonies and the fight against racism in the British context. *Race Today* also took energy from C. L. R James's principle that theoretical progress must be intertwined with grassroots activity, that activists had to connect with communities and to use their intellectual work to amplify the voices of the working-class communities in practical ways.

Race Today activists went from positioning themselves as immigrants, or children of immigrants, to identifying as British. This played a significant role in framing the rights of politically Black communities as a question of entitlement.

Race Today, September 1974.

Through their commitment to grassroots organising, the *Race Today* activists' attention was drawn to the housing crisis of Bengali families in Tower Hamlets and the growing numbers of families squatting in response. One of their key routes into the Bengali community came with the connection to Mohammed Ghulam Yahya, commonly referred to as Khosru Miah.

Before I met him, Khosru had been described to me by other participants as the 'Bengali giant'. He was taller than the average Bengali man; this, and his selfless support for many families, made him loom large in their memory. Now aged seventy-four he is well into retirement, and spends his time entertaining his grandchildren or at his local mosque. He explained that he came to squat after an older white man in the leather factory where he worked asked him why he constantly moved from one house to the next. Khosru had arrived in 1967. He was from Dhaka and came from an affluent and educated background. He had left Dhaka against his parents' wishes, yearning for the adventure of London. Leaving behind what would have been a comfortable government job, Khosru arrived in London and began working initially in a restaurant in Bishopsgate. He spent these first few years in shared rooms, sometimes 'doubling' to a bed – this meant that the bed was rented out on day/night shift basis and sometimes also meant co-sleeping – but he was constantly moved on when the landlords or sub-letting landlords needed the space, if someone closer in kinship arrived. Upon leaving the restaurant trade, Khosru moved into tailoring work and swiftly attained one of the higher paid roles as 'cutter'. It was while he was working in a leather factory that a white colleague, who noticed Khosru's housing predicament, took him to a vacant property and showed him how to break in:

I think it was 1970-something … seventy-something – I don't know. I hadn't heard of squatting before but there was an English man at my work, he told me, 'I'll show you how to get a flat – and you can have your own flat'. So he did the squatting for one flat for me. He showed me what to do. He just stood in front of the door and he hit it and it opened. There was a Yale lock, so he changed the lock and give me the key and said, 'This is your flat'. And he said, he told me that 'be careful – if you do this for other people, when you … open the door, straight away you change the lock otherwise there will be trouble'. I said, 'Okay'. After that I helped so many people, I don't know how many people, I helped so many people to get their own flat and all these things ...

It was a couple of years before his squatting activities brought him into contact with others who were also making a name for themselves in the Bengali community:

I'm not sure how I met Terry, I don't know, I can't tell you actually how I met Terry. Terence John Fitzpatrick his name is, I met him, and he told me all about this group. He asked me to go somewhere. When I go there, I saw Farrukh Dhondy, Mala Dhondy and Darcus Howe. So, we talked about these

Khosru Miah photo outside his home in Hackney © Seema Khalique.

things – I think there was a solicitor or somebody – so then we
decided to do something together for the Bangladeshi people.

Khosru's description of the ease with which he was guided to
squat stands in contrast with the years of housing hardship he had
experienced. He felt that the inaction of the housing authorities
regarding Bengali housing needs was embedded in racist indifference; this assessment forged his connection to *Race Today*. He
became good friends with Terry Fitzpatrick, Farrukh Dhondy and
Mala Sen and talked modestly about his 'community service'. He
argued that squatting seemed the only sensible measure to take
when the housing authorities refused to heed the housing needs of
the Bengali community, while at the same time boarding up and
deliberately damaging habitable properties. Their meeting initiated a new development in the Bengali squatting story, shifting
away from individual families approaching people like Terry and
Khosru, who were, by then, well-known squatters, to assist them
in finding a suitable property to squat, to the beginnings of a more
organised movement.

The *Race Today* editorial group, which began following the
Bengali housing crisis and the emerging squatter movement
from autumn 1974, started to document the housing struggle as
an ongoing series in their journal. They outlined their interest as
developing from stories that were emerging about housing discrimination. For them, the position of the Bengali community in the East
End was unique not because it was unusual experience for migrant
communities to experience housing discrimination – regrettably this
was the norm for most migrant communities in post-war Britain.
What was unusual was that the Bengali community were taking
direct action to bypass those systems of deprivation and violence:

> Asian families are not normally associated with squatting ...
> Nevertheless, as the pressure for accommodation grows in
> Britain's conurbations, workers both black and white are to
> provide their basic needs. Housing is one such, and in the
> East End of London a fringe of new immigrant families has
> been compelled to resort to squatting in order to have a roof
> over their heads.[16]

The article goes on to state:

> The decision to squat in such an area is both an answer to extreme need and an act of conscionable courage. The East End is not a friendly place, least of all to the eight or ten thousand Asians who provide the most recent recruits to the labour force of the traditional sweatshops of this dockland and commercial district.[17]

In the articles that follow, they relate how the struggle for housing was seen to be 'a fight for the preservation of community in which the social and political power of an immigrant force is based.'[18] In one of the first detailed articles in their monthly journal, they printed several accounts reported to them by the community. Two Bengali families were given council housing in predominantly white estates, both found themselves victim to an onslaught of racist attack and harassment. Abdul Motim reported how, on the first day, his fifteen-year-old son had gone to the local shop and been set upon by a group of white youths who stoned and beat him. The incident, though reported to the police, was not followed up. The next day Abdul's brother was also attacked as he walked back from the local bus stop, again the police response was dismissive. On the third day his younger son, aged thirteen, was attacked on a local bus and was then chased as he tried to escape – the group of white youths caught up with him and punched and kicked him until he was unconscious. When the incident was again reported to the police, they were reprimanded for interfering in 'children's fights' and warned to go home and stop making trouble. The article goes through several other stories, each one horrific for the level of violence and police indifference that is described. The article reports that, having exhausted efforts to ask the council to rehouse them or for the police to intervene, the families decided to abandon their prized tenancies and found empty properties in Spitalfields where they could squat.[19]

Khosru talked about that violence with ease – he was witness to and victim of such attacks himself. Something about the way he spoke seemed to indicate that the violence he experienced was so endemic to that period that it had become normalised. He recalled a time where he was attacked outside the London Hospital one night in the early 1970s as he was returning home from a restaurant shift on Christmas Eve:

> I came out on Christmas Eve, I came out – about 11 o'clock I reached Whitechapel, because my flat is behind the London Hospital. About 11 o'clock I came to Whitechapel, and I was walking on the street, and then two gentleman came … and that time I was young as well – two gentleman came – when they come in front of me and then both of them went on either side and then I realised that somebody was going to hit me. So one of them tried to hit me, but when he raised his hand – before he hit me, I hit him and he fell. I – I got hold of his neck, then all of them came out from the Brady Street and they beat me and one of them he had a knife and he tried to stab me and I got hold of his knife and was cut here [indicates his hand where there is a faint scar] and a little bit of it cut my belly. So there was a nurse, I think, coming out from working at London Hospital and she started screaming and they run away, and she's the one who took me to the hospital.

Khosru survived that attack with stitches to his hand and abdomen, but the violence was not just aimed at those on the street. Like the examples described previously, violence was regularly visited upon Bengali people in their homes, both because of a general hostility towards Bengali migrants but also when white neighbours came to realise a Bengali family might have audaciously taken a council house for themselves through squatting:

> There was one family, we squatted that family in the afternoon – we moved him there. And then by the evening he rang and straight away all of us go and get him out of there, and when we go there we saw so many stones in his house – all his glass [windows] are broken … we went and rescued him and after that I think we put him somewhere in Christian Street or somewhere, I don't know – I can't tell you exactly in details, it's quite a long time ago. But that's how we used

to face the racialism and every time – in one building if you saw two or three Asian people, there had to be some problem there.

As stated already, the act of breaking windows was not an organised racist campaign. However, it was universally translated as an act that denied the Bengali family the safety and privacy that was sought in a home. In this particular case, Khosru and the growing group of squatter activists were able to help the family to retrieve their possessions and relocate to a different squat.

Mala Sen was critical to many of the negotiations that happened between the collective and the growing numbers of squatter activists. She had travelled to the UK in 1965 with Farrukh Dhondy, who she had met at college, and who had been given a studentship to study in Cambridge. Upon arrival, the pair had together become activists in the Black Power movement, but as a woman who could speak Bengali, Mala was key because she gave *Race Today* the ability to communicate with the wider Bengali community in the East End. Meanwhile, as a woman she was also able to navigate the gendered divisions that regulated communication outside of the family for many Bengali women. She often responded to 'call-outs' when families came under threat or asked for housing assistance. In a news documentary from the time she said: 'It is an emergency situation where emergency action has to be taken, and when we talk about moving such families out – it has to be done literally within twenty-four hours'.[20] In this interview she goes on to talk about the choices Bengali families had: to either accept tenancies in areas where the family was likely to be subjected to racist harassment and violence, or to squat in the dilapidated confines of Spitalfields where the Bengali community was most concentrated. Sen's comments highlight that squatting was not just a way of appropriating a physical home – it was also fundamentally connected to the ability to feel safe.

The *Race Today* collective was involved in providing lawyers to advise on the legalities of squatters' rights. Migrants also found support from the Tower Hamlets Law Centre, who made clear to Bengali families that a medieval law dated to 1381 called the

Forcible Entry Act made it illegal for anyone to break in and evict them as squatters. *Race Today* provided practical support too by helping to move families and furniture into vacant properties and assisting with connection to gas and electricity lines. In the period between 1975 and 1976, hundreds of Bengali families were moving into empty houses on Varden Street, Walden Street and Old Montague Street. Admittedly, most of the properties were in poor condition, but even then, the properties remained valuable real estate. The properties on Varden Street were, for instance, owned by the London Hospital and they were due to be sold to the council on terms of vacant possession. Therefore, when the Bengali squatters moved in, this blocked the sale of the properties. In a bid to get them out, the council and the hospital conspired to make conditions difficult for the squatters: they had the gas and electricity board cut off supplies to all the properties.

Race Today, June 1976. Courtesy of the George Padmore Institute.

Like the family that they rescued and re-squatted in Christian Street, Khosru recalls that he, Terry and Mala were commonly called out to defend families experiencing harassment. Terry

Fitzpatrick was critical to the relationship between disparate groups of Bengali squatters and their ability to come together in the loose network of affiliation generated by *Race Today*. Terry was of Irish heritage but was born in Liverpool in 1946. He joined the army as a fifteen-year-old and after leaving he became a builder. He moved to East London in 1974 to join friends squatting in Stepney, before moving into his own squat at 12 Aston Street. He is widely acknowledged as a key member of what became known as the Tower Hamlets Squatters' Union. As a builder he was able to support new squatters as they opened up properties by helping fix them up. As a squatter himself, he also understood their legal standing:

> ... by certainly the end of 1975, certainly, the police have given up being aggressive. Very often they wouldn't turn up if somebody phoned up and said, 'Oh, the squatters have broken in', they'd just say, 'It's a civil matter, we've got better things to do'. There were too many. What's happening, it's happening every day somewhere in Tower Hamlets – somebody was breaking into somewhere and moving in a mattress, and then my rule was: get the door open, get the kids, the pots and pans and the mattresses, get them in. That's it – we're in. Occupation. Put the sign on the door and just stand your ground at the door. Doesn't matter who turns up – civil matter, go away. And the GLC might come around and say, 'Oh, you've got to move' and people would say, 'We're not moving', and that was it.

Although a white man, Terry was cognisant of the racialised dynamics involved in the housing exclusion that Bengali families faced, but his commitment to their cause was not inspired by Black Power politics; rather, it was a pragmatic defence of their right to housing. His lynch-pin role with *Race Today* was fraught with complexity and tension – he and Darcus Howe were far from friends and Terry was disparaging of Black Power politics. In fact, decades later Terry went on to be convicted of racially aggravated harassment against Lee Jasper, a prominent Black politician and activist. However, in the 1970s Terry was someone who was on the ground and was trusted by the Bengali community because he had helped so many of them to squat. While he was not sympathetic to the politics of *Race Today*, he was nevertheless pivotal to the interaction between them and the Bengali squatter community, and it is quite likely that had they not had his support, much of the squatter organisation that developed would have floundered.

By the middle of 1975 there was an increasing number of families squatting, which was beginning to attract some attention. Terry remembered:

> It was like guerrilla warfare. People would just say – they'd come around and say, 'Oh, what we're going to do?' I'd say, 'Break in, change the lock, put this sign up. Any problems, give us a ring. Okay?' But by the end of 76, the council's just given up. They didn't – they didn't even try to meet anyone. It was just – just trying to get their own tenants in as quickly as possible.

Individual squatters were becoming bolder, and in the summer of 1975 the first mass squat took over a row of empty houses in Old Montague Street in one fell swoop. Twenty-two adults and fifty children who had previously been deprived of council housing took their situation into their own hands. These families were no longer conducting this occupation in a secretive style; there was a burgeoning confidence, and the neighbouring streets were also soon taken over. With the numbers of squatters growing, their vulnerability to council harassment and eviction also diminished.

THE TIGER IS ON THE LOOSE

On Friday, 6 February 1976, what had essentially been a disparate group of squatters loosely organised around informal migrant networks formalised into a more coherent movement. In that meeting, Khosru Miah, Terry Fitzpatrick and the *Race Today* activists came together with dozens of other Bengali community members – many of whom were already squatters – to discuss the ongoing housing crisis and its racialised origins. It was here that the name Bengali Housing Action Group was suggested and immediately the connotations of the acronym BHAG, a term which in Bengali can mean both 'tiger' and 'share', was celebrated for the radical and collectivist traditions it denoted. At this meeting a simple constitution and executive committee were agreed. The constitution set out to campaign for fair housing policy for Black and Asian people. This was articulated in several specific demands which related to the most immediate concerns of the seventy-odd Bengali people that came together for the meeting. First, they argued that Bengali families should be given access to good quality housing and not 'low demand' properties, which were also usually those in the worst condition, where white tenants had been decanted from. Secondly, they defended the rights of Bengali squatters to access gas and electricity supplies. Quoting Tony Benn, then Minister for Energy, they argued that squatters were legally entitled to utility services to their squatted homes, and that the council's aggressive tactics of cutting off supplies was illegal and must cease immediately. In making these claims, the *Race Today* journal wrote,

> BHAG is a rejection of the solution to housing problems that the state has posed in other communities ... solution[s] which reduce the black worker ... to a wage labourer with no rights in the society and no claims on decent housing. The black workers of Britain have consistently refused to accommodate to this battery chicken model of a labour force. For years the British state has bought immigrant labour on the cheap, dodging the necessity to house, to skill and to reproduce the black labour force from conception to retirement. The presence of organisations such as the Bengali Housing Action Group, begins to put an end to this evasion.[21]

Khosru was one of the original members of BHAG. In his interviews he was clear that Bengali families squatted not just because of housing deprivation and the availability of empty properties, but because like Kadir and Sufia, they believed they were *entitled* to that housing. One of the most ostentatious of those claims was made after the conclusion of BHAG's very first meeting. Terry had spied an empty block of flats through the Montefiore Centre windows and suggested that a group of them go and have a look:

> As we're sitting there, I spotted this empty building out the back, so when we'd all finished we went and walked round. There was six staircases with ten or eight habitable flats on each one, and about two or three tenants left. So then we started getting lists of people, started organising and getting building materials together. And Farrukh and I and a few others, we broke in with the first six families on Easter Saturday 1976. Within six weeks, maybe eight, the building was full.

The building was called Pelham Buildings and came to be known as BHAG's fortress. It appears in the 1978 documentary *A Safe Place To Be*, where long, sweeping shots of the building with a low camera angle make the tenement block loom ominously. Clare Murphy, Terry's partner and a youth worker at the time, recalls that the GLC-owned building was empty because the previous, mainly white working class tenants 'had fought to get a compulsory purchase order on the grounds it was unfit'. Health and Housing Management Committee reports from 1972 detail tenant deputations raising 'bad staircase lighting, dumping of furniture, infestations of fleas, rats etc ...' as part of their campaign for wholesale rehousing.[22] But despite these obvious issues, Terry recalls, 'It was heaven for your family ... it had an inside kitchen, a toilet. The gas, water and electricity were on ... I mean as far as Bangladeshis was concerned, Pelham Buildings was ten times better than living on some estate in Poplar.' His words reiterate the safety element that was so highly prized in a home, especially at a time when attacks on Bengali families isolated on all-white estates was an everyday occurrence. Terry and Khosru thought that at its most populous, about three hundred Bengali people squatted in Pelham Buildings, and it is considered to have been the largest squatted settlement of its type.

Pelham Buildings. From *A Safe Place to Be*, by Simon Heaven,
Compass Films 1980 (BFI archives).

Mohammed Matin, who squatted as a young man in Pelham
Buildings, explained how important Terry was to the movement
generally, and in the securing and operation of Pelham's 'fortress':

> … people would go to him and he would help them find
> a place. There were about fifty, sixty, maybe seventy flats
> [in Pelham Buildings], and they had a kitchen, one sitting
> room and there were different sized ones. And he knew how
> to do jobs, and he knew people. He could change the locks,
> he would connect you up and he would make sure everyone
> had everything they needed. And everyone who asked, he
> would make sure he would find them something. By the end,
> there were hundreds of us in that building. I was a young
> man at the time and so I couldn't get a squat by myself, but
> my friend's family, they were really old – they were like my
> *dhadha* [granddad] and *dhadhi* [grandma] – and they needed
> help, and they asked me to stay with them – they used to be
> scared a little because obviously they knew they had broken

in to stay, so they wanted someone to stay with them. And that's how I stayed there in Pelham Buildings. So there was a system; we made sure that it was families that would stay, we made sure they got the flats first. We did better than the housing system! They wouldn't give you a flat for five or six years. Here we did it ourselves and we made sure that the list was that families and old people got the flats. We did it in a really nice way.

Mohammed Jashimuddin also squatted in Pelham Buildings. He, his wife and infant child occupied Flat 220 on the third floor, which he remembers needed significant repair when they first entered in 1976. Until 1971, Jashimuddin had been training to be a doctor in Germany – his father was part of the Pakistan foreign embassy staff based there – but Jashimuddin's life-course was suddenly changed when his father received news that all the male members of his family had been shot dead as part a Pakistani crackdown signalling the beginning of the war between East and West Pakistan. His father had a heart attack after receiving the news and passed away shortly afterwards. Jashimuddin was made aware that the Pakistani government 'did not want any Bangladeshi or East Pakistani domicile officers to remain in critical positions throughout Bangladesh or for the Pakistan embassy'. He recalled that the Pakistani ambassador stationed in Germany was sympathetic to his family's sudden and tragic plight and suggested Jashimuddin take up a less controversial welfare position in London on behalf of the Pakistani embassy so that he could at least secure a stable income for his family. Within six months, and with the emergence of Bangladesh as an independent country, Jashimuddin was working for what became the newly formed Bangladesh High Commission in London. He went on from this initial welfare role to serve as an official for the Commonwealth Service for another forty years, before retiring recently.

Squatting in Pelham Buildings required Jashimuddin to learn all manner of new skills:

My friend Rafiqul Islam who was in the other building – he was occupying the ground floor flat – he helped me do the wallpapering in the flat, and we went and we got from Sunday market some cut piece of remnant carpets. I just laid it there so that there was no dust there was, just for that purpose – that was it. We had a kitchen – a very small kitchenette with one ceramic sink, very old, which is now coming back in style. It was one little squarish or rectangular sink. And we had bought a second-hand cooker and I went to the Sunday market and I got one of those rubber pipes. And my friends told me, 'Look, you got to put something like a paste on the end so that it seals and you take a spanner and you plug that in into the gas thing and you plug the other hole into the cooker end and you light it and the cooker will work.' And it worked! It worked! I still remember it was one of the shops that sell – that sold a lot of hardware things. So I had to explain to the man, I need something to connect my cooker from the main organ pipe into the ... So that's how he gave it to me. This is Sunday market where we would go and buy our halal chickens, we will go and buy our vegetables and things. When you cross the road, you had Sami and Salim selling ... where we would go and buy our clothes, baby clothes, bed clothes, etc.

Even after fixing it up as far as he could, the flat was far from ideal for him and his young family, and he explained that whilst he could have chosen to find accommodation elsewhere because of his reasonably paid job with the High Commission, he felt it was part of his duty to ensure he was embedded within the Bengali community that he was there to serve:

We lived with fear of our life, lived with all the challenges, lived with all the difficulties. Imagine living in a place where you don't have any glass in your window and in winter cold air blows in, the rainwater comes in. You don't have a hot water. You have to boil hot water in a big pan in order to not only have your cup of tea but also to wash your children, wash your baby. These are no mean achievements. These are very hard things. Mashallah. We come from a very respectable family in Bangladesh. I didn't have to do that. I had a choice. I had a choice, but I forego the choice because I felt if you want to be a leader, you have to be with the people.

Despite all the hardship, Jashimuddin also recalls that the time he squatted in Pelham Buildings is also one of those he and his wife most often reminisce about fondly:

They were very happy memories. My wife and I often talk about those times that we spent. We couldn't have done on our own that is for sure, had we not had the support of the entire Bangladeshi family. Those families were like our own brothers and sisters and extended family because we all wanted to understand the welfare of each other. And that's how we survived this process because we stayed united. We stayed united.

Jashimuddin lived in Pelham Buildings for the entire time it was squatted by BHAG, serving as one of the Joint Secretaries of the organisation, and was the final squatter to be rehoused out of there in the late 1970s. He was aware of the building's long history and recalled through paperwork that came to him, that the original name of the building was the Schwartz Building. Terry also recalled first arriving with Bengali squatters and noticing that 'every single doorway had the mezuzah'. He said, 'When the Bangladeshis got settled down, they said, "What's that? What's that?" So I've got a screwdriver and prised it off, I've opened it up and shown them it's Hebrew – Jewish writing'.

The mezuzah may have been left by tenants long gone by the time the Bengali squatters moved in, but it was a poetic reminder of the importance of doorways as thresholds of encounter. Elizabeth Alexander's work on the mezuzah and the 'construction of social spaces in antiquity' explores the way that '[P]racticing the ritual of mezuzah was one way of negotiating the meaning of the built environment ... in arbitrating the boundary between inside and outside and in giving meaning to space on either side of the boundary'.[23] This symbol on the front door of each flat was not only a reminder of communities of people that had moved through these spaces before, but also hints at the ways that those communities might have practiced rituals that 'stake[d] a claim for Jewish presence in the public spaces of a multicultural urban environment'.[24] Many decades later, Bengali migrants were claiming that same space through a very public display of squatting.

Reviewing this early part of the development of the squatter movement, Sarah Glynn concludes that Bengali involvement in *Race Today* was 'pragmatic rather than ideological', and that there was little intellectual synergy between Bengali squatters and the Black Power politics of *Race Today*.[25] While it does appear that many squatters were indeed disinterested in the revolutionary politics of *Race Today*, squatting can itself be seen as an act of defiance that is saturated with political purpose, even where that purpose may not be openly articulated. bell hooks defines resistance in a way that does not require a conscientious and deliberative act of defiance. For example, she registers the act of care that a Black mother performs '[i]n the midst of a brutal racist system, which did not value black life' as an act of resistance, concluding that, '[t]hough black women did not self-consciously articulate in written discourse the theoretical principles of decolonization, this does not detract from the importance of their actions'.[26]

Whether it was my parents, who stayed on as uncomfortable squatters, or those like Khosru who were actively supporting hundreds of families to squat, Bengali squatters were occupying and squatting properties that the GLC and Tower Hamlets council were egregiously withholding from them on racialised terms. They were looking to survive in a system that denied them the social resources to do so. There were people like Abdul Kadir, who challenged the housing deprivation they experienced, took what they felt they were owed and quietly supported others around them to do the same, and Sufia, a young migrant mother who defended her squatted homes against those who sought to evict her family. Like the Black mother bell hooks describes who, in the act of holding and caring for her infant, resists a racist system bent on destroying her family, Bengali squatters were creating their own 'subversive homeplace'.[27] These ideas are explored further in the next chapter, moving away from the squatted dwelling to squatter vigilantism and the claiming of home in the *para*.

NOTES

1 The estate name has been changed to protect the privacy of this participant.

2 Deborah Phillips, 'What price equality? A report on the allocation of GLC housing in Tower Hamlets', *GLC Housing Research and Policy Report 9*, Greater London Council, 1986, p28.

3 Charlie Forman, *Spitalfields: A Battle for Land*, Hilary Shipman: London, 1989, p56.

4 Kathy Burrell, 'Spilling over from the street: Contextualizing domestic space in an inner-city neighbourhood', *Home Cultures*, 11, 2015, p152.

5 Tower Hamlets Local History Library and archives, ref: LCX00001, newspaper cuttings file.

6 *Credo*, LWT, 1978. Available at: https://player.bfi.org.uk/free/film/watch-credo-1978-online.

7 Pete McGuire, Susan Daniel, Pat Doyle, *The Paint House: Words from an East End Gang*, Penguin: London, 1972.

8 Paul Dimeo, 'Colonial Bodies, Colonial Sport: "Martial" Punjabis, "effeminate" Bengalis and the development of Indian football', *The International Journal of the History of Sport*, 19(1), 2002, p83.

9 Ibid, p72.

10 Georgie Wemyss, 'British Indian seafarers, bordering and belonging' in *Routledge Handbook of Critical Studies in Whiteness*, Routledge, 2021, p255.

11 Gurminder Bhambra, 'Colonial taxes built Britain. That must be taught in lessons on Empire', www.opendemocracy.net, 1 April 2022.

12 Geoff Dench, Kate Gavron, Michael Young, *The New East End: Kinship, Race and Conflict*, Profile: London, 2006, p207.

13 *Race Today*, Vol. 7, Issue 9, September 1975.

14 The death of two-year-old Awaab Ishak in Rochdale in 2022 due to similar conditions of damp and mould illustrates that these issues persist for working-class people in the UK. See Mark Brown, Robert Booth, 'Death of two-year-old from mould in flat a "defining moment", says coroner', www.theguardian.com, 15 November 2022.

15 Paul Field, Robin Bunce, Leila Hassan, Margaret Peacock (eds), *Here to Stay, Here to Fight: A Race Today anthology*, Pluto Press: London, 2019, pp10-11.

16 *Race Today*, Vol. 6, Issue 9, September 1974.

17 Ibid.

18 Ibid.

19 *Race Today*, June 1976.

20 Thames Television, Racism East London: Asian community: Our People, 1978: https://www.youtube.com/watch?v=Eyuw50IYk4A.
21 *Race Today*, Vol. 8, Issue 3, March 1976.
22 GLC, Health and Housing Management Committee Report, 1972-1973.
23 Elizabeth S. Alexander, 'Ritual on the Threshold: Mezuzah and the crafting of domestic and civic space' in *Jewish Social Studies: History, Culture, Society*, Vol. 20(3), 2014, pp100-102.
24 Ibid, p107.
25 Sarah Glynn, *Class, Ethnicity and Religion in the Bengali East End: A Political History*, Manchester University Press: Manchester, 2014, p22.
26 bell hooks, 'Yearning: Race, gender, and cultural politics' in *Hypatia*, Vol. 7 (2), 1992, p46.
27 Ibid.

3

Safety first: Squatters
secure the streets

In September 1993 I was in the second year of my A Level
studies at a local sixth form college in North London. Outside
of lessons I spent a lot of time in Lucky 7, the local pool and
games hall. One of the top ten hits of that time was Shabba Rank's
'Loverman'. It was played incessantly and my friends amused
themselves by changing my name to 'Shabba', pronounced the
way it is in the song. I had moved to further education from an
all-girls secondary school where I had experienced, for the most
part, the benign neglect of teachers, in what I quite early on came
to understand as racialised, class-based and gendered understand-
ings of what I was capable of and destined for. I was a Bengali girl,
part of a large community of working-class Bengali families in
and around the Kings Cross area at the time, and we were expected
to get married at the age of sixteen and stay home to start our own
families. To be fair, this was an expectation that was common in
our families at the time. Our teachers, assuming this was our prescribed destiny, did little to nurture our educational ambition.
My view of the world was intimately and self-consciously connected to this intersection of race and gender and was shaped by
what I detected as my differential, and most times inferior, treatment based on those identities.

I remember feeling comfortable for the most part in my home in
Hackney. The low-level mindfulness of having to dodge eggs that
were sometimes thrown from the top floors of the old people's home
that I walked past on our grocery trips to Ridley Road Market, or

the continued but irregular knock-down-ginger 'antics' at our front door, did not register as grave, physical threats of racist violence. But the mood music to the 1990s and my late teenage years was turning, and was beginning to feel decidedly more sinister. In April 1993 eighteen-year-old Stephen Lawrence was stabbed to death by a racist gang as he waited for a bus in Eltham, south-east London. A few months later, a little closer to home, a seventeen-year-old Bengali boy, Quddus Ali, was out returning a video rental to a local store in Stepney Green when he was set upon by a group of eight white racists who beat and kicked him unconscious, leaving him in a coma for four months suffering life-changing injuries. Two days later, local communities gathered for a vigil on the steps of the London Hospital where Quddus was being treated. His mother spoke in Bengali to the crowd, inviting their prayers and support for justice. What started peacefully slipped into violence as flyers thrown at the police by a handful of young Bengali men initiated a full riot police response resulting in dozens of injuries. In the aftermath, nine young Bengali men were arrested and charged with rioting, though these charges were later dropped or reduced.

Even though I had little contact with the Bengali community in Tower Hamlets at that time, I could feel the angry shift among young people; our usual discussions in college shifted from the banal to include talk about what was happening in the neighbouring borough and our own experiences of racism in Hackney. The rise of street violence was tightly tethered to the rise of the British National Party, a far-right party whose headquarters were in Welling, near where Stephen Lawrence had been murdered. Its leader, Derek Beackon, was elected as a local councillor in Tower Hamlets' Isle of Dogs eight days after the attack on Quddus. His victory came as a shock but in reality was made possible by a local political context where racialised divisions were actively stoked by mainstream parties like the local Liberal Democrats. The BNP stood for what they described as the 'real British people' and had the repatriation of Black and Asian communities as one of their key manifesto aims. In the glow of his post-election victory, Beackon described Bengali people as rubbish that he wanted to sweep from the streets and he made housing allocation one of his key priorities. The weeks and months that followed witnessed violence reminiscent of what my generation had only heard described to us by our parents, including one occasion where white youths rampaged down Brick Lane smashing windows and shop-fronts. There were huge demonstrations against the BNP organised by the Anti-Nazi League and a famous demonstration of over 50,000 people to close down their headquarters in Welling. For the first time in my life I was seeing a level of racist violence that made the streets seem like a threatening place. I was also older and more able to critically engage with media coverage that lamented the tragic attacks on Stephen Lawrence and Quddus Ali but simultaneously blamed the young 'rioters' who had come out in retaliation. It was also inescapable that the police appeared on so many of these occasions, including the Welling demonstration, not simply to be inert in the face of the security threat experienced by Black and Asian communities but actively defending racists in their violence. Derek Beackon might have promised to 'take our country back' but for many of my generation, we were reminded of the need to secure our streets, neighbourhoods and council chambers from a racist threat that many of us had felt, perhaps naively, was receding.

*

For Bengali migrants, 1970s London was often a dangerous place. Bengali squatters reached out to secure the surrounding streets and neighbourhood in response to the violence they encountered both at the thresholds to their homes and in the wider community space. There was therefore a clear (though not exclusive) link between Bengali squatters and the development of vigilante groups that sought to defend the wider community against racialised street violence. With the support of *Race Today* activists, Bengali squatters began to organise themselves into self-defence groups that challenged police failure to protect the community, not by insisting on better policing but by bypassing them entirely. The experience of direct action in housing led many to believe that state institutions would not understand and cater for their needs, and that mobilising the community's collective power was a better way to secure their safety. In many ways the activity in the mid 1970s provided the impetus for, and nurtured the capacity of, the

Bengali community to mobilise after the 1978 murder of Altab Ali. It also helps to explain why this moment of community anger was able to coalesce so powerfully at what became a turning point in East End social history.

Bengali squatters were concentrated in a relatively small area in Spitalfields and Whitechapel, but this *local* fight for home, or *para* (neighbourhood), was situated within *national* racialised geographies of 1970s Britain, which fixated on a narrative that migrants were a drain on social housing. Bengali families were often squatting in houses and flats that were unfit for habitation, which meant that they had to reach out beyond the home into their immediate urban environment in order to perform everyday domestic tasks like bathing and showering. The wider *public* neighbourhood therefore had to fulfil some of the purposes associated with the *private* home. On the one hand, these were culturally familiar homemaking practices for Bengali migrants, for whom the public-private differentiation as it is constituted in many Western societies is anyway incompatible with the extended space of the home in a South Asian context. However, when transposed into 1970s East London, these familiar practices became dangerously charged events. The impact of these encounters was highly gendered; for male migrants who had previously enjoyed *para* as a type of parochial space, even an extension of their home-territory, 1970s Tower Hamlets was an acute deprivation of that spatial liberty and mobility. In some instances this street racism led to resistance, but who fought back and how was intersected by generation. It was primarily younger men and boys who organised patrols and fought back, and who nurtured something of a diasporic identity, while older men tended to adopt a more restrained attitude, namely because they remained committed to a return 'home' to Sylhet. It was this generational aspect, rather than colonial tropes about the passive, 'effeminate Bengali' activated in the press, which determined whether and how Bengali migrant men were prepared to fight back.

There was a clear gender division too, and although there were occasions that Bengali women joined in the more visible, street-based demonstrations, traditional gender norms generally dictated that few women were involved in patrols. The generational dimension was also an important intersection here; female Bengali migrants were usually young mothers and had familial caring responsibilities, and although Bengali women were threatened with and did experience racist violence, especially in the threshold spaces of their home, the street patrols that emerged were mainly to safeguard against the dominant form of male-to-male violence in the street, and it would have been unusual for women, either white or Bengali, to have been involved in street-fighting.

SPILLING ONTO THE STREETS

Spitalfields has often been described as an area on the edge, a space of negotiation between the 'included' and the 'excluded'; from French Huguenots in the seventeenth century to Irish Catholic migrants in the early eighteenth century and Eastern European Jews fleeing pogroms in Russia, the area has often become home to people on the move. Each of those communities endured their own tensions and hostility despite sometimes romanticised accounts that herald the East End as a sanctuary for successive generations of migrants. In the 1970s the junction of Brick Lane and Bethnal Green Road was precisely such a margin; the National Front relocated its East London branch office to the Carpenters Arms pub in the mid 1970s and would sell their newspaper *Combat* under the railway arches at the north end – just a few minutes' walk away from BHAG's new fortress in Pelham Buildings. Two other pubs further along the Bethnal Green Road, Blade Bone and the Salmon and Ball, 'stood as guardians of white supremacy.'[1] These pubs and the newspaper pitch marked a frontier space beyond which Bengali migrants feared for their safety – a space that rose to notoriety for coining the term 'paki-bashing'. Christopher Husbands uses the term 'racial vigilantism' to describe how the National Front policed the 'boundary' between Shoreditch and Bethnal Green Station and the junction with Brick Lane; Husbands argued that there were effectively 'no-go areas' for Bengali people and that the railway bridge towards the north end of Brick Lane was precisely that edge.[2] This was not to suggest that Bengali migrants were significantly safer on the other side of that railway line – the National Front went on violent sprees up and down Brick Lane on more than one occasion – but Husbands' idea of a boundary function between these areas and the pattern of racial attacks are important to understanding how Bengali migrants experienced the different geographies of their neighbourhood as hostile or relatively safe.

The GLC, which owned the majority of the properties in the area along with Tower Hamlets Borough Council, had emptied out slum housing with the ambition of future redevelopment. However, with budgets tight, these plans had failed to materialise, leaving scores of empty, boarded-up properties. At times, the council would deliberately vandalise and wreck the plumbing and heating systems in the houses and flats in order to deter squatters. Most Bengali squatters came to occupy the empty properties within a close geographic area in and around Spitalfields and Whitechapel. The public bath system, which had been a lauded advancement in public health in the Victorian era, was by the mid 1970s a fading norm as bathrooms were built inside newer homes. However, for Bengali squatters (and indeed even those who did get tenancy, since mostly they were allocated the oldest, most rundown properties), the lack of internal baths in these properties required them to perform this intimate task in public space. Significantly, the nearest public baths were in Bethnal Green and Poplar, areas that were well known for being racially hostile and would normally have been avoided.

In Sylhet most people grow up bathing in the *phooshkoni* or the *phokoir*, a freshwater pond located in the *bari*. All the Bengali squatters I spoke to who arrived as migrants were accustomed to these public bathing spaces. However, in contrast to the use of the *phooshkoni*, which was considered a fully functional, freely available part of the stretched home, even a space for sociality, visits to the public baths in East London were compromised by the regular and routine threat of racialised violence and required collective planning ahead of a visit. The use of public baths in this sense generated the need for solidarity among men in a way that differed from the way in which they would have used the *phooshkoni* in Sylhet. This experience of hostile public spaces in turn created the possibility for organised resistance. For Bengali men, being 'at home' in Sylhet had involved unrestricted mobility, with safety assured in the extended home space. The Bengali squatter vigilantism that emerged in the form of patrols could therefore be seen as an effort to recreate that sense of 'home territory', in defiance of racist violence.

Gedu Miah, while not a squatter himself, was a supporter of BHAG. Initially he started off helping other families by 'opening up' empty properties so they could squat, but eventually, like others, his activism evolved to include a wider security role for the community. Gedu came to the UK in 1968 aged eleven with his mother and three older brothers. He began by living in Birmingham. His father and paternal uncles had all worked in factories in the city and his grandfather before them had served as a sailor in the British Navy. Therefore, although Gedu may have been a new migrant, his family's lineage and their settlement in the UK was intimately tied up with colonial and post-war Britain.

Gedu was a youthful-looking sixty-three-year-old man. When we first met he wore a short leather jacket that sat just below his hips. He was neither freshly shaven nor did he court a traditional beard. He had a catchphrase that he repeated periodically in the interview: 'It was not easy Shabna, life was not easy'. One particular episode of 'life not being easy' that he described to me haunted me for days after our interview. It was not related to housing, nor did it take place in East London, but it epitomised the complex and cruel ways that racism manifested for many Bengali migrant children. It also highlighted the courage it took to survive in these insidious systems of violence. Gedu said:

> In my school – I think I was the second Asian, there was one Indian boy and myself, and we both were in the same class, but unluckily I can't even speak Hindi at that time. We had a lady teacher… on one Friday, we were about to go home – school had nearly finished – and she got so fed up, she got so fed up because kids are making hell of a noise. One of the white boys beat up the Indian guy so the Indian boy went to tell Miss – 'Terry beat me'. That was the white guy's name – I still remember it. He said, 'Terry has beat me up', so she called Terry and Terry went to her and said, 'No, no, it wasn't me – it was Gedu'. So she called me up, she knew it wasn't me and because I couldn't say anything – and even though the Indian boy was saying, 'It's not him', she made me bend over and she

hit me so hard with the board, even though we all knew it wasn't me and that Terry had beat up the Indian boy. She hit me so hard, so many times. I got really, really upset – so I said, 'Bloody hell', I said to myself, 'What's going on?' It doesn't matter whether I can speak or not, no one is going to do this to me anymore. From Monday I went in and went straight up to the white boy Terry, I don't know even know how I said it but I said, 'You're not gonna do that to me again because if you do, I'm gonna beat you up so badly'. He didn't do anything to me again. But the teacher – she got away with it.

Gedu's parents were upset by the encounter but like lots of Bengali parents they were ill-equipped to deal with the English schooling system and advised their son to keep his head down and get on with his schooling instead. The family did not stay in Birmingham for very long. Gedu's father lost his job in the factory so the family moved to London. His parents decided to retire to Bangladesh a few years later, and Gedu decided to stay on in the care of his three older brothers. By this time the brothers were in Spitalfields and were fortunate to rent a small flat on Hanbury Street, which they shared with other single men. Gedu recalls negotiating with his father before he left:

I don't like, you know, sleeping with anybody. I wanted to sleep in my own bed, so when – before I moved from Birmingham I said to my dad to tell my brother that I'm not going to share with anybody, and I want do my own thing. So they said, 'Okay, you can sleep in the single bed in living room.' And there was a very tiny, tiny, kitchen where you had the cooker – the sink being shared by two flats – and the toilet was outside. There wasn't a hot water system. You know the old paraffin heater? I don't know if you remember, the old paraffin heaters. Every Thursday … a big lorry comes in, knocks on the door – 'paraffin man, paraffin man' … It was a hard life, you know, people sharing beds, no space.

Gedu acknowledged that he was fortunate – he and his brothers managed to rent a property, albeit one with no heating or hot water.

But even imperfect solutions like this were not guaranteed. The council not only neglected the Bengali community's housing needs, they had a policy of surveillance and harassment whereby they hounded men living in shared accommodation like Gedu by using 'health and safety' and legislation that prohibited overcrowding:

> In my room there was another two people, on a sofa double bed. So you know when night times comes, you just open it out. You know, it was really hard … almost every other night a council environmental health officer comes and checks how many people lives there. So if there is three beds in this house, three people have the night dress on – but there were eight or nine people living there, but the other has the trousers/shirt so on. So the health inspector comes in and we say, 'They're guests – they don't live here, okay?' And once everybody is ready to go bed – it doesn't matter who knocks the door, you not going to open it. But some people would open and then were caught and were fined. It was hard – hard for people to find a place to live, and they did not make it easy for us.

Despite the 'luxury' of having his own bed, the flat did not have hot water or a bath, so Gedu was forced to use the public baths in areas that he otherwise knew not to go to. The men in his house would make sure they planned their trip to the baths so that they could go in groups and avoid being alone. Mashuk Miah, introduced in the previous chapter, also talked about how visits to the public baths had to be carefully organised. Mashuk had a clear idea of the racialised geographies of the streets in his neighbourhood, and his comments indicate the strategies he and his friends would develop to navigate their way around the risks that this manufactured:

> When we stayed in Pedley Street, in Wheeler House, at that time half of Brick Lane was the Asian people's, we could use it regularly, and half – from Pedley Street, from there to Shoreditch, from that side – the white people, young whites, they used to trouble our people – we couldn't go that way. If we even went that way – and we had to go that way because of the baths – at that time there weren't baths inside, baths

were outside – what was it called? Cheshire Street. There was
a bath there, we used to go to that one – it was near our
house. But you would always get into a fight. Every Saturday
or Sunday – Sunday was market day, and there would be
fighting. We needed to go, we had to go to the baths, we had
to go, and so we would go as a group. If we went as a group
they wouldn't trouble you, but if they found you as one or
two they would hit you, they would ask you for what was
in your pockets. One time there were four girls – girls! They
surrounded me and said, 'What's in your pocket? Give it'. I
said, 'Girls! Want what's in my pocket? No, no!' I chided them
and they went. But it was all the time, all the time, so you
never went alone.

Mashuk had arrived to join his father as a 15-year-old boy and
had, throughout his childhood, enjoyed roaming his Sylheti village
freely, being at leisure to wander local *baris* and even going considerable distances into the local *bazar*. Bathing was a social activity
and had involved extended periods of playfulness with other boys
and young men. But living in 1970s East London posed a significant challenge to this spatial cultural heritage. The racialised access
to the neighbourhood decided the routes that were taken. Mashuk
and his friends developed a colloquial map of the area, generally
avoiding going beyond the railway bridge near the Bethnal Green
end of Brick Lane, except for these otherwise unavoidable trips to
the public baths.

In 1976, Luqman Uddin was fifteen and squatting with his
family (pictured below). He had originally arrived to one small
room above a restaurant on Grays Inn Road. His father, who had
been in Leicester for some years, had recently migrated to London
looking for employment in the garment industry. Luqman arrived
along with his mother and younger brother and, struggling to
find accommodation, rented a single room above the restaurant in
Kings Cross. The overcrowding and shared facilities with several
other families and the restaurant staff were, he said, 'intolerable',
and to ease the burden the teenage Luqman was sent to stay with
a *mama* (maternal uncle) in Tower Hamlets. It was on a journey
with his *mama* to new job in an embroidery factory on Cable Street

From right to left: Luqman Uddin, his late mother Komla Bibi, younger brother and late father, circa 1978. Personal photograph.

that they spotted the boarded-up flats on Fieldgate Street. Luqman recalled knowing that a lot of Bengali people were squatting and he claimed there was little controversy over the decision to tear down the boards of a flat and reunite the family in one space. The flat was in dismal condition; there was no gas or electricity connection and, like another participant Maryum who squatted with her parents as a much younger child on that same street, they installed a shower that hung over the toilet, which meant you had to close the lid of the toilet to shower over it.

These washing facilities were grossly inadequate and, like Mashuk and Gedu, led Luqman to the public baths and into racially hostile situations that he might otherwise have avoided:

We went to public baths: Poplar had baths, Poplar Bath, Hackney Bath – public bath. So once a week we would go to the public bath. At that time – if you think about my Amma and other family, they didn't know English or English society, they had not adopted it, and so it was very difficult. So they would somehow manage a bath at home. And also, on top of that, you had racism near those baths: the whites didn't like us and would swear at us and they would attack us. We would attack them too, from time to time ...

The accounts here point to just how hostile the neighbourhood, or *para*, usually experienced as an extended home space for men in Sylhet, became for Bengali men in 1970s East London. Luqman noted vaguely how his mother would 'somehow manage a bath at home'. Most female participants did indeed bathe at home and this too brought its own hardships.

Whilst women in rural Sylhet would have experienced a significant degree of 'spatial confinement' in what Shayer Ghafur from Dhaka University describes as the wider 'urban public realm', they would have enjoyed substantial freedom of movement within the 'inner zone' of their *bari*, and would have experienced the courtyard as an open and accessible space for a variety of shared household chores.[3] As Iftekhar Ahmed, also at Dhaka University, has noted: 'During the day, the courtyard becomes the territory of women because most of the men are away working in the fields or outside the homestead. In addition to various household activities women also visit neighbours and spend time in their courtyards, unhampered by the presence of men during the daytime'.[4]

The village as a space of work and leisure extended to bathing, which was also a sociable activity. Rarely did women bathe alone. Komla Bibi was Luqman's mother and can be seen with her young family in the photo above. Komla would have bathed with her female family members and fellow villagers back in Sylhet and would have been able to enjoy socialising in that segregated space. Komla's fears of racist violence and the restrictions they implied for her freedom of movement were clearly painful in her early migration experiences; she had moved from a spacious *bari*, with networks of solidarity and care in the form of her daughters and her wider family networks, to a confinement that was contoured not by gender norms but by the threat of racialised violence.

Komla was in her eighties when I interviewed her and has since passed away. I visited her at home, a new flat in a mixed tenure development just off Aston Street. In the late 1960s and early 1970s, Aston Street was at the heart of a white Tower Hamlets squatter collective. It was also where Terry Fitzpatrick had begun his squatting career, going on to become one of the community's key supporters. Komla, though herself a squatter, was unaware of this other history. She sat on her bed for our interview and asked me several times about my marital status, enquired about the number of children I had, and told me I looked like one of her granddaughters. After establishing I was the mother of two children, she was curious about why I would be spending my time asking about a house she had lived in forty-five years ago. When pressed, she said she did not recall much about it: 'It was a broken house', there was nothing more to say. 'We broke in – everyone was doing it,' she said matter-of-factly. What did emerge from our conversation was that she found the threat of racist violence a serious impediment to going outside and to her sense of wellbeing:

> There was so much fighting. The English – they couldn't stand to even look at us! But Allah sorted it out! There was so much fighting. I was so scared, I used to stay at home all the time. I couldn't even take my children to school – their father used to take them. I was too scared, it was lots of *bera sera* (winding routes). I didn't like to go out at all.

Komla went out very infrequently and only when she was with her husband. She recalled spending the early years after migrating here crying constantly and wanting to go 'back home'. She had left two daughters – Luqman's older sisters – in Sylhet because they were not classed as dependants by the racialised and restrictive immigration rules at the time, and she felt enormous sadness for their absence and for the wider family network she had left behind. She never visited the public baths; she had a tin bath at home and would fill it up with water boiled on the stove.

Hajera[5] was a child when she squatted with her parents in Spitalfields. She recalled a 'grey iron, freestanding tub' which had appeared in her childhood home and recalled:

It was really hard to have a bath – I remember the very first time somebody had a bath in that building, it was quite a novel thing – bit like having a TV in the mid 1980s: you would know which home had a TV set. So, I remember that we didn't have a bath – that was quite difficult – and then we had a bath and that was seen as a luxury in what was then a condemned squat. It was squalid basically [laughs] but as a child you don't know what is squalid and what isn't so you just think: this is home.

She recognised in hindsight the 'squalid' nature of her family's squatted flat and how as a child her reference points were so limited that this had just been 'home'. Now in her late forties, she recalled a recent event she attended which reminded her just how skewed her perspective had been at the time:

I was watching a film the other day in Mulberry School, they had made a story about Aldgate with local residents who had lived in the area for the last seventy, eighty years odd. And there were lots of Jewish families who were in their eighties talking about the first time they had a bath in their homes. That was actually in the 1940s. I was describing the bathtub coming in late 1970s so just imagine the levels of poverty there – that people tell you about their stories of poverty, but they are probably my grandparents' age, and we had to live through that poverty in the same way and find our way out of that. So that – that always makes me reflect a little bit because whenever you hear people tell stories of poverty, they're often telling stories of when they were younger – seventy years ago – but we experienced that poverty and that very deep poverty in my lifetime, with my parents, and it wasn't my parents' poverty alone, it was ours as well, but you don't realise that until you're a little older and you start reflecting back on all of that.

Hajera's positive memories of the arrival of a tin bathtub in her squatted home and the later realisation that this reflected a level of poverty that she had not been able to register at the time offer an important insight into the levels of hardship experienced in Bengali squatted homes.

Husnara, just a few years younger than Komla and a widow of some fifteen years, had a more positive experience of the push beyond the home that came with the deficiencies of her squatted house. Husnara came to squat near the London Hospital in 1975, on a street that became part of the BHAG squatters' network and which was home to many other Bengali squatter families. Husnara and her husband arrived in London in 1972 as employees of the Bangladesh High Commission. Both were educated and Husnara had accompanied her husband on several foreign postings before coming to London. In 1975 her husband and many other colleagues at the Bangladesh High Commission were 'let go', ostensibly because of a change in the political administration in Bangladesh after the assassination of Sheikh Mujib, founding father of the Bangladesh independence movement and the country's first prime minister. The family moved from West London, where they had resided while he was a High Commission employee, and tried to find accommodation in shared spaces. Unable to secure accommodation, they heard about people paying 'key money' to what she called 'hipsy-tipsy' white squatters on Maynard Street,[6] who were moving out:

> … the English were selling up, and they weren't real English people – they were hipsy tipsy, you know, so many different people, they stayed ten-twelve people to a house. They would leave the house for £200, £100 for a house. For them, they had stayed for free, but now that slowly their comfort was reducing, they slowly began to leave. At that time £200 was the equivalent to £10,000.

They paid £400 to the not 'real English' white squatters to obtain the key to a property where they then became the squatters. She recalled how her family were the first Bengali family in the street, but within months all the white squatters had left and Bengali squatters had moved in. This was likely one of the turning points in the character – and colour – of squatters in the area.

David Hoffman's acclaimed photographs document these so called 'hipsy-tipsy' white squatters. For Alexander Vasudevan, author of *The Autonomous City: A History of Urban Squatting*, these 'misfit squatters' were experimenting with 'alternative political identities and subjectivities'.[7] In many instances these squatters dominate the popular imaginary of what squatters in 1970s London looked like. Yet for Husnara and other Bengali squatters, these white squatters were peripheral to the Bengali housing crisis and the squatters' movement that developed from it. For a start, though there was some resentment at white squatters jumping the housing queue, there was no fundamental objection about their right to be housed; they were generally considered part of what Professor Bridget Anderson calls the 'community of value', or the 'good citizen', who is essentially entitled to the provisions of the state.[8] This was quite unlike the state and street racism that denied the legitimacy of the Bengali community to be in East London in the first place, let alone have a right to social housing.

Husnara recalled the violence that saturated her everyday reality:

> When we first arrived it was like a jungle! The skinheads – *hai*! They used to give us trouble. After dusk we couldn't go out of the house, they would hit and grab us – our sons in particular. If our sons went out they would hit you, tear your shirt, hit and beat you, take your watch, your money, whatever you had – or even if you didn't have anything, they would beat and leave you ...

Husnara had no bathroom in her squatted home, but in addition to that her family had no gas or electricity – the houses had all been disconnected from their suppliers. It was common practice for the GLC and Tower Hamlets Council to do this, despite it being illegal. The reversal of this practice was one of BHAG's main campaigning goals. Many Bengali squatters like Husnara faced considerable hardship, enduring long cold winters in dilapidated properties where, despite establishing billing accounts and sometimes being able to restore services intermittently, they were deliberately harassed by the council, who would instruct suspensions of service:

> We used to use paraffin heaters, using paraffin – that's how we lived. What choice did we have? There was no electricity

– and it was so smelly, the whole house. So much work and suffering. I stayed here for six months burning candles, I had to stay like that, and I'd go and cook elsewhere – there was no gas either – I had to go out to cook. There were a few houses on Romford Road, some people I knew with gas and electricity, so I used to go and cook there. I would go in the morning and cook and come back, I'd buy candles and water bottles on the way home. But when you were out, there was always danger. There were skinheads. We all had to fight – even us – we would, when they attacked. I would grab a rod and go out. And quietly, when the police came, we put the rod discreetly under the car. We had so much trouble!

Unlike 'public' bathing, which might have been culturally familiar, cooking in traditional Bengali homes was normally located inside at the back of the *bari*, and was performed exclusively by women. In 1970s East London, performing her domestic duties as a Bengali woman brought Husnara into contact with the wider neighbourhood in ways she would not have experienced in Sylhet, as she was compelled to make regular trips outside the squatted home to be able to feed her young family.

In her account she also speaks about the racist violence that she witnessed and her intervention in at least one incident. Her experience is markedly different to Komla, who found the push outside of her home distressing and frightening. Husnara, on the other hand, whilst lamenting the routine violence experienced by young men, found it positive that squatting made it necessary for her to be out in the wider neighbourhood. Taking her cooking outside of the home brought her into contact with other families, and she framed her day around school drop-offs and cooking in other people's homes. Meanwhile, she was also taking on home-garment work and filling her day with activities, supporting other women with trips to the hospital or to access health care services. In some ways squatting allowed her to connect with others in her community in a way that she may not have if she had access to gas and electricity.

What these varied accounts indicate is that the material deprivations that many Bengali migrants experienced in their squatted homes required them to navigate areas of their neighbourhood which they otherwise might have avoided. There were clear zones within which the Bengali community knew they were at more or less risk of racialised violence, and while in the main they would observe those boundaries, many Bengali squatters had to access those 'boundary' areas in order to do basic, everyday tasks like bathing and cooking. This exacerbated the racialised violence they experienced and exposed the failures, and indeed complicity, of the police.

'WE DON'T WANT NO PAKIS HERE'

The term 'paki-bashing' first came to prominence in early 1970, when local and national newspapers began to report the increased racialised violence against the Bengali community in East London. On 5th April 1970, the *Observer* noted that 'any Asian careless enough to be walking the streets alone at night is a fool'.[9] Tosir Ali, who was walking home alone on 7 April 1970, was attacked just after midnight while returning from his shift as a kitchen porter at a Wimpy Bar in the West End. He was stabbed in the throat by two men, who ran off and left him bleeding. He dragged himself up six flights of stairs before collapsing at the front door of his third floor flat in Bow. While the *Observer* lamented the foolishness of Bengali men walking alone at night, Tosir Ali, like many others, had few options but to work a low-paid job with anti-social hours; walking home alone at night was an unavoidable occupational hazard. Later that month about fifty white youths stormed down Brick Lane, smashing shop windows and attacking people on the street. In the police action that followed four people were arrested: two white youths and two Bengali youths. The latter were charged for carrying weapons while the white youths were later let go.

Racialised violence in the 1970s was not an aberration but symptomatic of and legitimated by the highly racialised national politics of the time. Enoch Powell's 'Rivers of Blood' speech, delivered in 1968, reflected the idea that Britain was essentially white and that the safety and security of British identity relied on excluding and limiting the presence of 'alien' Others. As Stephen Ashe, Satnam Virdee and Laurence Brown have argued, rather than 'paki-bashing' being the 'sport of choice for the extreme Right or an anomic and lunatic minority', it was integrated and enabled by a political context that presented immigrants as a 'threat to an imagined white British society'.[10] In an infamous television interview for 'World in Action' in January 1978, Margaret Thatcher, then Conservative Party leader and leader of the opposition, used calculated language when she referred to a fear that newcomers with a different culture would swamp Britain. This rationalisation of racism gave license to street violence against immigrant communities. These interactive and mutually constitutive layers of racism rested on a deliberate colonial amnesia that erased the long connection between the Bengali community and East London, which starkly contrasted with the way that community understood both their presence in, and entitlement to, that area and its resources.

The summer of 1976 was unusually hot. My mum recalls being cooped up in the house on Deal Street with me – a new-born baby – and a pre-school child, with no access to family networks. Outside the door lay a landscape that threatened eviction and simmered with racialised violence. The *Race Today* journal that year documented the violence that accompanied life for the local Bengali community. Mustafa Siddiqui, a young Bengali man working part-time in a tobacconists on Brick Lane, became involved in a squabble with some white customers over some sweets. Alerted to the altercation, another group of white youngsters entered the shop and stabbed Mustafa in the shoulder. The commotion that ensued attracted a fractious crowd and the police later arrived on the scene. They detained both Mustafa and the young man who had stabbed him and put them both into the same car. Witness statements were taken and the weapon was retrieved by the police. Later that evening police officers visiting Mustafa in hospital advised him that the case should be dropped and the attackers should not be prosecuted, in the interests of 'racial harmony'. The Siddiqui family refused but despite insistent follow-up calls to the police station, no further action transpired.

That same month Maklis Ali, who had been allocated a tenancy by the GLC on the Mountmoress Estate on Commercial Road, was greeted by a hostile 'reception committee' as he arrived with his family to take up residence in his long-awaited council flat. In a situation that was not uncommon, the all-white estate residents gathered to prevent them from entering their new home. The crowd of women and men wielded sticks and iron bars, shouting 'we don't want no Pakis here'. On the front door of Maklis's new flat was a painted sign that read: 'No Pakis here. Vote for NF'. The police arrived but refused to intervene and instead advised the family to go back to the council and ask for a transfer else-where. In another housing-related incident, Matasin Ali and his family were ambushed in their GLC flat in Hollybush Gardens. The family had been subjected to harassment by young people on the estate: their windows were constantly banged on, people would urinate on their front door, their washing was ripped off their washing line and they were regularly subject to threats and abuse. The fifteen-year-old child was regularly beaten up, several times in incidents involving knives. On the 14 July 1976, the family were subjected to a prolonged ambush as bricks and stones were thrown through their windows by a group of white youths that had congregated outside. Calls by others to the police to intervene were dismissed by the police responder saying they were dealing with burglaries and did not have the capacity to respond. In the event it was BHAG activists that came along to chase away the attackers and rescue the family, who had been trapped inside for six hours.

It was not only a case of police indifference and neglect; on many occasions the police actively participated in racist violence. In one event, Bethnal Green police officers broke down the door of a first floor flat in Arthur Deakin House. A Bengali family had entered and squatted the night before and the estate residents were unhappy about the situation. They and the caretaker of the estate had called the police, who then proceeded to illegally and forcibly evict the family. When BHAG activists went along to the police station to complain about their illegal actions, the inspector replied that the families were fortunate not to have been arrested for threatening behaviour. The racialised violence of housing deprivation and the failures of the local police were intimately linked, and together interacted to prevent the growing Bengali community from feeling at home.

Chunu was a key member of the Bangladesh Youth Association that formed in 1976 primarily as an organisation delivering recreational opportunities for Bengali youth, who were excluded from other provision. Chunu was not himself a squatter, but like many other young men at the time his activism was multi-focal, and his own housing hardship and his support for others brought him into contact with BHAG. Chunu migrated to the UK in 1969 aged eleven with his mother and three siblings. Up until then, he and his siblings had lived among a large, multi-generational extended family in a village *bari* in Sylhet. His father had moved to the UK in 1957 and worked regularly at the British Leyland factory for some years. In 1969, earlier than many other families, his parents had decided that it was a good idea for the family to come and join him, and Chunu along with his mother and siblings left Sylhet for Birmingham. However, a few years later his father was made redundant and they decided to move to London, with a view to the sons finding work. Chunu remembers leaving what was a big, four-bedroomed house with a garden in Birmingham to come and live in a one-bedroom flat in Tower Hamlets owned by an uncle, who had just bought it from a Jewish landlord. The family applied for council housing and waited for years but were only offered accommodation in areas they could not contemplate living in:

> We were there quite some time because I remember dad made an application and the place they offered after a few years it was like Poplar, places that dad did not want to go. The reason was there was a lot of racism, lot of abuse, and you were picked on. So there was – there were certain places that he was like, 'that's a no-go area'. Nobody wanted to go to Bethnal Green. Nobody wanted to go to Poplar. Nobody wanted to go to Wapping. It was basically – the choice was made that there are more Bengalis in E1 so don't go out of E1. It was because he thought we were a lot safer … All you heard in those days was … someone got beaten up because he lives in Poplar. Or, someone got beaten up because he lives in Bethnal Green, or

that the whole block is all white and there is just one Bengali family. It was ongoing every single day, every single week, it was endless. Some friends I had, they would go to work, and their place was broken into during the day. They started carrying all their valuables with them to work, but that wasn't safe for them either. That's just how it was.

Chunu left school and got a job in a tailoring factory on Commercial Road. He recalled the street racism they experienced at the time and how getting to work and back, or even any attempt at leisure time, was animated with danger. Many of his friends had 'a curfew put on them because their parents – they were so scared about what would happen if they were out at night. We literally couldn't go out of the house'. He recalls that going out alone at night was unthinkable: 'You were not safe. If you came across one individual or a single person you might be alright, but if you came across a group then almost always they would give you a good hiding'. He described settling into his life in London:

> Call it a man-made jungle or whatever. I mean literally back home you can, when you're bored, you can go out because you live in a village and you can run around – here you couldn't. You couldn't even open the door and leave without fear, so it was more like a prison than a life.

Chunu's description of his arrival to a 'prison'-like space was repeated by many interviewees and contrasts greatly with the memories of the *para* that they had enjoyed before migration. The Bangladesh Youth Movement that he founded, along with others like Jalal Rajonuddin, reflected this wider aspiration for safety, but also spoke to the yearning for recreational space and the ability to relax and enjoy sport and cultural pursuits.

Jalal Rajonuddin (pictured below) had a similar story to Chunu. He had arrived as a young boy in 1972, just after the Liberation War. He had started off in Birmingham before moving to London in search of better prospects. Both his parents retired back to Bangladesh but Jalal stayed on, moving around various shared accommodation in Tower Hamlets.

Jalal Rajonuddin in *A Safe Place to Be* by Simon Heaven,
Compass Films, 1980 (BFI Archives).

He too described how the 1970s were fraught with violence, and how national and local level racist politics interacted:

> ... following on from Enoch Powell's speech – rivers foaming with blood – there was paki-bashing that was widespread throughout London and the country. The momentum was there for the racists to make the lives of Bengalis and other ethnic minorities a misery, and that's what happened. I mean, I remember the period when people used to go out only in groups so that if they came under attack they could try to save or defend themselves. That's how life was. The community was under siege.

He recalled one time he had been bold enough to venture to a travelling funfair that had arrived in an open green space called Bigland Green and had been set upon by a group of white boys, who had punched and kicked him until he was unconscious. He awoke later in hospital to find out he had been rescued by Caroline Adams, author of *Across Seven Seas and Thirteen Rivers: Life Stories of Pioneer Sylheti Settlers in Britain*, who was a youth worker at Avenues Unlimited at the time. Jalal's housing hardship brought him into contact with Terry, Khosru and Gedu, and though he didn't squat he stayed in The Hostel near the Tower of London, which was a space where he met other housing activists.

Both Chunu and Jalal's perspectives were interesting because they both highlighted how narratives of exclusion relied on blaming Bengali migrants for the victimisation they experienced. Chunu recalled:

> All these councillors, they would come on TV and they were just very negative, you know ... portraying the Bengalis in this way – that they don't know how to live, they don't mix with us, they don't talk to us, you know? It was always about *us* not integrating and not settling in, not anything to do with *them* not giving us the chance to settle ...

Bengali men were said to be cowardly because they didn't fight back. They were thus regarded as alien to the rules of brutish masculinity that dictated the dynamics of space in 1970s East London. Joseph Hunte, the local Chairman of the Citizen's Committee of Tower Hamlets (CCoTH) at the time, even stated:

> I get the impression that the West Indians are quite liked. Their language and behaviour patterns are the same. But the Pakis [sic] are introspective and more remote. And they are never willing to resist. If the skinheads tried it on West Indians they would give them a rough old tumble.[11]

This divisive narrative played on the idea that the West Indian community was both more culturally assimilative and aggressive, in contrast to the Bengali migrant who was both culturally alien and passive. Both tropes are damaging and were rooted in colonial narratives designed to suppress resistance and secure colonial power through dividing communities. There were some older

Bengali community members who did indeed counsel against fighting back and relied on negotiations with the police and local council. In the documentary *Credo* (1978), Gulam Mustafa, then Secretary of Brick Lane Jamme Masjid, set out the rationale for this by saying:

> We are peace loving people, we are not violent. And also people feel they are here in this country to work, earn their living and learn the skills and do as best as could possible, being a representative of their country, like an ambassador.

But what Gulam was saying here was not that Bengali migrants were innately passive, but that they were effectively transcontinental commuters who were preoccupied with returning home. In part this ambition was rooted in the historical context of newly independent Bangladesh. For these older men, still tied by their remittance responsibilities and extended family at home, they imagined they were going back to Bangladesh to nourish their newly founded independent country. On the other hand, the younger generation took inspiration from the Bangladesh liberation movement to nurture their activism here, both in terms of squatting and the wider vigilante patrols that emerged.

'IN BANGLADESH THERE WAS ONE WAR, HERE THERE WAS ANOTHER WAR – AND WE WON THIS PLACE, WE CLAIMED IT'

The Bangladesh Liberation War loomed large in the minds and memories of many participants and would frequently emerge in ostensibly unrelated conversation. As part of my research I spent time at various day-care centres in East London. On one occasion I was engaged in a light-hearted conversation with a group of older women. They were sniping about younger Bengali women, who they said walked about like they were *beta manush* (men-folk), carrying big bags, always out and about with no restrictions. We all laughed when I picked up my rucksack and I pointed out that perhaps they were referring to me. They reassured me that they were obviously not because I was 'carrying important books' and 'completing important research'. The women continued laughing, moving on to talk about marriage proposals and scoffing at young women who were supposedly refusing good marriage offers. As the conversation flitted around these generally playful generational injunctions, a woman called Lutfa[12] who was sat next to me started talking about her marriage and the death of her husband at a young age. Our conversation shifted away from the jovial banter that was being batted around the room as she began telling me her unusual migration story.

Lutfa had arrived in London as a twenty-year-old widow in 1972, raising her children here as a single mother. Her husband, a *Londoni*, had travelled to Sylhet to accompany her on her scheduled journey to join him in London, but his return was mistimed with the outbreak of the war. He could have returned to London but Lufta was pregnant and he insisted, despite the family's counsel and pleas, that he would stay. Just a few weeks into the war he was rounded up along with all the young men in their Sriramishee village and shot by a Pakistani military unit in the courtyard outside the main line of *baris*. She recalled returning to the village to see dead bodies scattered across the courtyard. Her father-in-law was one of the older men who had evacuated to the jungle area with the women. He returned with her and, in shock at seeing his dead son, fell face first into the dirt. Lutfa's most vivid memory was not the bodies – these were indistinct in her mind – but her father-in-law's front teeth embedded in the ground, angled and protruding from the hard soil. The teeth remained in the ground for weeks afterwards, a gruesome reminder of the war crime that had taken place there.

Shortly after the birth of her son Lutfa used the papers that had been arranged by her husband to come to London. Her own father and uncles were all in London and had shared accommodation with her now deceased husband. They decided that it was better that she use her immigration papers while she could, before any further restrictions could jeopardise her right to travel to London. She raised her infant child and two older children as a single mother and never re-married. Lutfa's story was not unique, but I remember it well because of the way it juxtaposed with the light-hearted conversations just before it. Many participants had equally tragic and violent memories of this period. Even for those not directly involved, the war featured strongly in explaining their loyalty to Bangladesh.

The nine-month Liberation War was rooted in much longer legacies of British colonialism, including the partition of India in 1947 to create the Muslim state of Pakistan. This newly formed state was divided between East and West Pakistan, the two regions separated by 1600km of Indian territory. The relationship between the two territories was, from the outset, characterised by inequality. The western wing assumed dominance, despite East Pakistan's demographic majority, and ruled with poorly disguised economic neglect, political discrimination and cultural marginalisation. When the results of an election in 1970 gave East Pakistan and the nationalist Awami League Party, led by Sheikh Mujib, a parliamentary majority, the West Pakistani leadership refused to relinquish power. Instead, it launched a military attack that culminated in what many have described as attempted genocide.[13]

The popular narrative about the war for those from East Pakistan revolves around the brutal violence that many experienced first-hand, where a powerful military was pitted against an unarmed civilian population. However, the story is also rooted in the longer history of cultural and linguistic oppression that triggered the Bengali language movement of the 1950s.

After a stumbling start, with allegations of inefficiency and corruption as well as international interference, Sheikh Mujib, the first Prime Minister of Bangladesh, was assassinated in 1975, heralding the beginning of regular political and military disruption in the subsequent decades. The way that people talked about their transnational relationship with *Desh* was underpinned by these, at the time recent, events. It was clear that Bengali migrants carried something of the political and cultural inheritance of this activism into the way they understood their marginalisation in 1970s Britain and their divergent responses to it.

Although the attempted genocide inflicted by the West Pakistani state and military are clearly different from the state and street violence experienced by Bengali migrants in 1970s postcolonial

London, there are certain threads of the experience that resonated with squatter activism. The racism that Bengali migrants experienced in London relied on presenting the Bengali community as 'alien' and 'inferior', which was evocative of the disparaging and discriminatory treatment of Bengali cultural identity by West Pakistan. This discrimination played a significant role in mobilising the Bengali community in the lead up to the 1971 Liberation War.

Jalal was involved in vigilante patrols in and around Tower Hamlets. He reflected that this transnational historical context was important, arguing:

> People like me who came to this country at the age of twelve would have remembered the War of Liberation in Bangladesh. I, and my family, and my generation, supported the independence of Bangladesh. A new identity, in a sense our own identity of belonging to a community, having the right to speak our own language, I think it must have played a role in giving us the strength and the impetus for our movement or fight for our survival in Tower Hamlets.

Jalal Rajonuddin, October 2022. © Seema Khalique.

Husnara was the mother of four daughters when she began squatting. She also explicitly linked the housing struggles Bengali migrants faced in the East End and the Liberation War they had just fought in Bangladesh. Husnara repeatedly talked about fighting to stay in this country and identified some inheritance of the Bangladesh conflict in the 'war' they faced here:

> We all had to fight, even us [women] … we had so much trouble, but we even enjoyed that fight [laughs], if I'm honest, we enjoyed that fight! Life was sad and happy, so much *khosto* (hardship). In Bangladesh there was one war, here there was another war – and we won this place, we claimed it.

In our interviews Husnara's loyalties oscillated between the local, the national and the transnational. Her stories were littered with references to Bangladesh, and her patriotism adorned the walls of her home in the photographs and *nakshi* (a specific style of Bengali embroidered tapestries) that were proudly displayed.

Husnara in her front room. The wall features family photos and posters of Sheikh Mujib and Sheikh Hasina. Photograph by the author, August 2020.

When asked about the role of women in the squatting movement, she compared the domestic work she undertook to make the
dilapidated squatted home habitable for her family, and suitable
as a meeting space for male squatter activists, to the work Bengali
women performed during the Liberation War to support the *mukti
bahini* (freedom fighters). Husnara recognised that in both events
women's labour may not have been the centre-stage activity making
headlines or being captured in photographs, but she insisted on its
value as a contribution. The work women performed, work 'that
you may not see', was pivotal to the success of both movements,
she argued. She recalled, for instance, the time and effort she spent
cleaning the soot stains from her squatted home that climbed the
walls and ceiling, and the care taken to make it habitable for her
young family. 'Could we have lived there if I didn't do that', she
asked rhetorically, 'of course not!' Her words resonate with the
conclusions drawn by Professor Yasmin Saikia, who argues that
there has been 'gendered silencing in the sites of history'.[14] She
highlights the way that 'official' histories of the 1971 War, for
example, have suppressed women's experiences and contributions.
For Husnara, the women who fed the freedom fighters that hid
in jungles during the war were making a contribution to the war
effort. She compared this with her feeding the people who would
gather at her squatted house to organise collective responses to eviction threats and write letters to the council. Husnara also related
how she personally visited the utility company offices and negotiated the reinstatement of gas and electricity lines when there was
official pressure on such companies to refuse such squatter requests.
Her words hint at how women were involved in grounding their
families and community through the reproductive and domestic
work that they performed.

Ashfaq was a young boy when his family squatted in Varden
Street. His family had been in Dhaka during the beginning of
the war. His father, a diplomat, had been stationed as part of the
Pakistani Diplomatic service in Hong Kong, but just before the war
he had been posted back along with all other Bengali employees.
His father was then imprisoned for the entire duration of the
fighting. Ashfaq, who was eight, took refuge with his mother and
two siblings first in his paternal grandparent's village and then in his

mother's natal village outside Komilla. He spent the war unsure of his father's fate and talked happily of the day when, shortly after the conclusion of the war, his father had come strolling down the main road leading into the village. He recalled feeling shy and relieved, hiding in the folds of his mother's sari as his father approached.

A couple of years later the family were posted to London and Ashfaq remembered with some horror the conditions of the houses they lived in – the High Commissioner's wage did not go very far in London. The family moved into East London, initially renting a shared room with another family before moving into a shared house. During these experiences he remembers his father meeting Terry Fitzpatrick, Farrukh Dhondy and Mala Sen. His father was educated and literate, quickly becoming a person who others in the community would turn to for assistance with their housing bureaucracy. This then linked him to other squatters, and in 1974 Ashfaq remembers the family moving into Varden Street, realising only much later that they had become squatters.

Ashfaq joined the Bangladeshi Youth Movement in 1978 initially as a social space, somewhere he could play football and cricket, but it soon became the place where he began to link his housing experience with the wider racism the community faced. He described the way that the 'big brother' types he met there understood their militancy and their demands for self-organisation based on two key principles, the first being that they were *British citizens* and that their labour, plus the labour of their fathers and grandfathers, entitled them to a safe and permanent home in Britain. Second, they actively linked their London-based political activism to the resistance of their forefathers in the liberation struggle. Ashfaq recalled:

At that time the youth – we were really politically active. Whatever the issue there would be lots of activity and demonstrations. I went back to the BYM just a few months ago and now it's just a club, it's somewhere people just hang out you know, and I think it's because they don't have those experiences to draw on, you know? In the 1970s there was that level of political activity around the Liberation War – there was those social discussions going on with the big brother types, and you know – you absorb that, don't you? So I'm glad I've had all those experiences because they helped shape my own life.

Nurul Hoque and his wife Anwara Begum were squatters in Pelham Buildings, BHAG's 'fortress', which was occupied in spring 1976. That same year, the couple also squatted a basement flat a short walk from Brick Lane, where they set up a Bengali language supplementary school called the East End Community School (EECS). Nurul and his wife were from Chittagong, a port city in the south of Bangladesh. The couple were well educated and had arrived in the UK so Nurul could pursue further study. Nurul and his wife both wrote and self-published memoirs about this period of their lives and Nurul appears prominently in the documentary episode 'Defending a way of life', archived at the British Film Institute (BFI).

Defence of the Bengali language was critical to the development of the Bangladeshi independence movement. The cultural and emotional attachment to language inherited from the events leading up to the 1971 War were clearly instrumental to Nurul's campaign to build the East End Community School and his efforts to mobilise wider community support for EECS as a Bengali language school in 1970s East London. Complaining about the racism and cultural alienation that Bengali children experienced in mainstream schools, Nurul argued:

> These realities of negligence and discrimination against our community compelled us to organise this school ... The school symbolises our cultural aspiration. We are British but we are Bengalees [sic]. The United Kingdom is our homeland. We are an integral part of British society but we want to maintain our cultural heritage and identity.[15]

Nurul makes reference to the UK as 'our homeland' but is also clear that this new place of settlement should respect the need for Bangladeshi cultural expression, specifically the transmission of the Bengali language, which had been at the heart of the conflict with East Pakistan. In another documentary, *Credo* (1978), Nurul went on to state:

We will not tolerate th[is] nonsense. We are the rightful citizens of this country. We are not ship deserters. We have not come here unlawfully. We have come here as a legacy of imperialism. We have come here ... legally. And we have been accepted by the ordinary people of this country. So we have nothing to fear. Nobody gives you freedom. You have to fight for it. Nobody fights for you. You have to fight for yourself. So we have accepted this lesson.[16]

Nurul directly refers to the 'legacy of imperialism' and finds in that relationship the legitimacy of Bengali people to make a claim for home and belonging in Britain, drawing on Sivanandan's now familiar refrain 'we are here because you were there'. Nurul speaks directly to the narratives of post-colonial erasure; even without the reference to 'ship deserters', his words demonstrate a clear understanding of the political discourse that sought to diminish the long connection between Britain and Bangladesh, and thus the rightfulness of their citizenship claims. The definitive call to fight for freedom, and a recognition that this is how rights are won, is evocative of his own activism in the events leading up to the Liberation War, including as an undergraduate student in the Bengali language movement in 1960s Chittagong. There is a clear inheritance of the activism *there* in how Nurul understood and resisted the racialised exclusion that Bengali migrants faced *here*.

Terry Fitzpatrick made the same link. His assessment of why Bengali migrants became key squatter protagonists in the 1970s relates back to both the tight-knit migrant networks within which they operated and the political attitude they brought with them:

... by the early part of 1975 ... I was starting to understand about Bangladeshi culture, about Sylhet. The Liberation War had just finished, I knew it had been a terrible thing, and what struck me was that was the resilience of these people. You know, you've, you've come out, first of all, a war, and then a monsoon and a typhoon in which 3 million people have died, and you're quite happily in the centre of one of the richest cities in the world moving into a state-owned house. Nobody worried about it.

Terry clearly references the close historical context of the 1971 War and the hardships people had suffered. For him, this and subsequent experiences had given Bengali migrants a 'resilience' and boldness that was quite unique. In another interview, he went on to make an even more explicit link between these experiences:

> For the younger ones, they imported the culture direct from Sylhet – they had just fought a war for their country against the Pakistanis and then they came over here and then took that fight straight to the streets here … So they had just had this whole fight against the Pakistanis who just committed brutal war crimes against them – they weren't going to come and just be pushed around all over again.

The inheritances of the 1971 Liberation War often coalesced with how younger Bengali migrants understood the racism they faced in 1970s London to create the impetus and inspiration for wider vigilantism. By the middle of the decade, the direct action that Bengali migrants took to house themselves was feeding into organised patrols that surveyed and secured the wider neighbourhood around the squatted community, bypassing the police, who were often as integral to racism as the council was to their housing deprivation.

'JUST PUT IT IN GEAR MAN AND GO, GO, GO …'

Helal Abbas arrived in London as a young boy and became the Secretary of BHAG at the age of seventeen. He was friends with Chunu and squatted in Nelson Street after experiencing a prolonged period of housing hardship where he and his family lived with more than a dozen others in a three-bedroom house. He recalled:

> When were in Chicksand House, we could see white families moving into newly built Kingwood House, and the empty house, dilapidated, old flats in Greatorex House or Chicksand House were reallocated to a Bengali family. It doesn't take a great deal of intelligence to figure it out – you can see the

pattern, the pattern of racism, the pattern of racist allocations was very obvious.

He was clear that home in 1970s East London was defined by the (in)security of the location and that the vigilante patrols which emerged in June 1976, shortly after the formation of BHAG, were a response to this wider insecurity. Describing his own experiences as a teenager, he said:

> People were seriously beaten up, people died. I remember going to school – the goal of going to school wasn't about how much you're going to learn that day, it was about how you can avoid getting bashed up and beaten. So the success would have been I got beaten less, beaten less today than the other day.

He also went on to recall that the need for self-defence was rooted in the neglect of the local police at the time:

> … because police protection wasn't there … the police never turned up. The police never took it seriously, and one of the justifications of some of the senior police officers was the police were a reflection of the society we live in, and that's basically saying well, if there's racism out there then there's racism in the police, what do you expect us to do?

For Helal, racist policing was intimately tied with his experience of housing deprivation and racist violence. In April 1976, an article in *Race Today* highlighted an episode where a Bengali squatter on his way to his squatted home on Old Montague Street was physically attacked by a group of fifteen to twenty young white boys. He was pursued by the group to his home where his wife, who heard the commotion and came running out, was also attacked. The boys only left when others from the street came out, but not until they had kicked the man unconscious and left his wife bleeding on the ground. The article detailed the indifference of the police and concluded 'where the lives of Bengalis are threatened and the authorities responsible are as slipshod as the police have been,

Helal Abbas in Altab Ali Park, October 2022 © Seema Khalique.

then physical defence is legitimate. Counter-attack is an equally legitimate form of defence.'[17] In a letter to then Labour Home Secretary, Roy Jenkins, they warned that 'our organisation intends to take full responsibility for the defence of our membership once it is established that those who carry that public responsibility fail in the job of protecting our lives'.[18]

Farrukh Dhondy was one of the signatories to that letter. As a *Race Today* activist and regular on the patrols, he was clear that squatting and vigilantism were intimately linked: 'It is not simply a question of homelessness … tied up in the fight for a decent home is a fight for the preservation of a community.'[19] In our interview he flicked through the archival material that I had collected, exclaiming with happy surprise at the articles he and others had written, which he had long since forgotten. Dhondy is now seventy-six years old. He is still very active and works on various media projects, for which he travels frequently between India and England. As a wealthy Parsi migrant, he arrived in the 1970s on a scholarship to study quantum physics at Cambridge University. At the end of his studies, he was reluctant to go back and 'make bombs for the Indian government', so he stayed in the UK, moved to London and joined the British Black Panthers. He described with relish the adventures he had with the activism of the group. After its collapse, he became one of the founders of the *Race Today* collective along with Darcus Howe. Dhondy made a clear connection between squatting, vigilantism and the securing of *para*. Like Helal, he talked about police negligence and even police complicity with racist attacks as one of the main reasons for resorting to direct action: 'Complain to the police? The police would laugh at you. "You got beaten up? Good. Show me the bruise – ha! I'll give you another one" – slap!'

By June 1976 *Race Today* were urging for the creation of what they called 'an alternative defence force'. They wrote: 'we put forward the strategy of organised and disciplined self-defence groups ... from within the Asian community. Their implementation is now urgent if the streets are to be made safe to walk on ...'[20]

Dhondy went out on the vigilante patrols and recalled the violence of some of their encounters:

> ... we started vigilante groups, you know that, to stop paki bashing, and we had fights. Terry was in one or two of them, I was in one or two of them, actual physical fights with guys who landed in vans looking for people to beat up. Then we said, 'Get back in your manor, fuck off from here' – you know, Khosru – he fought a lot – and actually maimed somebody [laughs]!

This was not just about claiming a home in the shadows of the most dilapidated properties in the East End but a claim to *para* around that squatted zone, where the Bengali community had begun to gather as protection against racist violence. He wrote:

> The Bengalis are victims only to the extent that they are in the process of becoming protagonists. Their self-activity on the housing front resulted in a large-scale squatting movement which in 1976, was transformed into a vigorous campaign around a demand for decent housing in the E1 area. Then in 1977 when white racists intensified their murderous campaign, a section of the community responded with an organised self-defence force.[21]

Dhondy's interview and archival writings suggest that, at least amongst the BHAG activists, there was a clear understanding that squatting and wider community safety were necessary to secure a sense of being 'at home' in East London. The success of squatting as direct action against institutionalised state racism was now twinned with direct action against street racism.

In another article from June 1976 they described the activities of the patrols:

> We've been told that a white gang gathers there around pub closing time. The Asian tenant who brings this information has had his windows smashed, his house robbed, his children assaulted the previous day. The buildings around have a long history of shameful racist intimidation abuse and assault. We are to go and talk to the Asian families on our rounds. Two of the families tell us, standing in their doorways (which we do deliberately to inform the neighbours of our presence), that the police have been called each time there is an assault, and each time they have carried away the Asian who complained and charged him. We suggest practical ways of collective self-defence.[22]

The article details the patrols that young men like Gedu, Khosru and Farrukh would make, along with Terry. Mala Sen, who was often a driver on these patrols, talked proudly of the direct action that was taken:

> We had the most militant wing of the organisations in the area, with the majority of the Bengali community in the area. We used to run patrol groups at night, vigilantes, to stop stray Bengalis being attacked.[23]

Gedu, who was in his early twenties by then, often went out on these patrols too:

> Squatting and patrolling they were at the same time – together – because every night people were getting beaten up by racists. In the seventies – now, you probably have two cars

in your house; you have one, your husband has one, or your daughter, son has one ... But in the seventies there was probably handful of cars amongst our friends. And I remember Terry had a Ford Zafire – it's a massive, big car – and we used to go out, eight or nine o'clock in the evening, for night-time patrols. We would stay near the underground until it closes ... We were patrolling the whole street until three or four o'clock in the morning – we did this for over a year! Over a year! Can you believe that? And it was seven days – every day we did it! One time me and him was going patrolling – and there was too many of them (racist white youths) and he said, 'You drive the car – I'll go and beat the shit out of them' – and I said, 'I can't even drive', and he said, 'Just put it in gear man and go, go, go!'

It would be a mistake to suggest that the vigilante patrols were entirely rooted in the squatter movement as there were many groups that emerged independently of it; however, squatter activism was, for many, the gateway into other forms of community activism. Gedu talked about the weekly clash between the vigilante patrols and the National Front, who had a newspaper pitch at the top of Brick Lane. Their presence was a source of huge tension and attracted a much wider pool of racists from outside of the East End, which often led to increased incidences of violence at the weekend. The market pitch was secured on a first-come-first-served basis, so many of the Bengali activists who were involved in beginning these patrols strategised that the best way to seize the pitch from the National Front sellers was to turn up earlier than them. Initially, they turned up as early as five o'clock in the morning, but retaliatory organising from the NF meant that in order to assert their claim to the pitch, Bengali activists began sleeping there overnight. Gedu remembered:

It wasn't easy. Every Sunday we have another problem: at top of Brick Lane, NF came in. They want to sell their paper and then come to Brick Lane and beat Bangali – Paki, you know. And sometimes, you have to defend, you know? Where we are at today, it's not been given – we had to demand and fight for it. We stood, we slept on Brick Lane on Saturday nights so the NF can't come on Sunday mornings opposite bagel shop to sell their paper. We occupied the whole footpath – we went in there, we said to some people, 'you stay there – when I've done my round I'll come and join you.' We would go there twelve o'clock. We put some people there and once we finished, we would go and sleep there. We made sure the National Front stayed on the other side of Bethnal Green Road.

For some of the older sections of the community, while the direct action iterated in squatting was seen as unavoidable and therefore tolerated, this street vigilantism was a step too far. Many had the mindset that they were here, as Gulam Mustafa, Imam of Brick Lane Jamme Masjid at the time had said, as 'visitors'. Other elders counselled that not only was vigilantism ineffective, it was also likely to jeopardise relationships with local political structures. In the paper 'Striking back against racist violence in the East End of London, 1968–1970' Stephen Ashe et al describe this split as the tension between the 'politics of convention' that sought to win change through navigating the system and those who shifted to the 'politics of the street'.[24] Younger Bengali men derided the faith that these older community members had in those systems as misplaced and an impediment to the community organising on its own terms.

For the *Race Today* collective this generational division was the source of some frustration. It is clear that some understood the reticence as certain elders in the community having been 'co-opted' into the system. There was scorn for the 'opportunist elements' in the community, who they described as 'middle class Asians, white left vanguard parties, race relations and labour movement hacks'.[25] The *Race Today* perspective was cynical about the support offered by these elements, arguing that they were designed to either appropriate the Bengali community's struggle for their own divergent interests, or that their appeal for moderation and working within existing structures was a threat to the militancy of the movement. Sarah Glynn's review of the period laments the failure of the Bengali movement to connect and find solidarity with the organised left, but *Race Today* activists and many of the younger Bengali activists viewed the International Socialist Group (later the SWP) and left organisations with some suspicion, and found the appeal to working-class solidarity incongruent with the regularised and brutal violence meted out by white people who were working class.[26]

With escalating levels of violence and damning evidence of police neglect, old and new Bengali community groups came together in an uneasy alliance in the summer of 1976. The Bangladesh Welfare Association, which had formed in the 1950s originally as the Pakistan Welfare Association, was by the 1970s a support organisation that was dominated by elders and more middle-class business leaders. They had traditionally advocated for working within the existing state structures but even they were now somewhat galvanised by the momentum that was gathering for more radical action. A local meeting was organised after yet another episode of violence where two young men leaving their factory shift had been set upon by a group of twenty-five white boys. The two were kicked, punched and stabbed, and little effort was made by the police to catch the perpetrators. On that same night a group of six Bengali men were arrested and detained at Bethnal Green Police Station on the basis that they were part of an illegal vigilante squad. They were released without charge but only once their passports had been inspected. The meeting discussed these incidents – not just the levels of violence but the failures of the police. In follow-up meetings a steering committee for taking ideas forward was established and BHAG members and *Race Today* activists were represented. The new organisation that developed was named the Anti-Racist Committee for the Defence of Asians in East London (ARCAEL).

This was, of course, at a time when few Bengalis had landlines so organising was done through word of mouth. ARCAEL called for a massive show of public rage at the increase in racist violence and the reluctance of the state to deal with it. There continued to be dissent – some of the older Bengali migrants counselled against taking direct action and were scornful of the radicalism of their younger counterparts. Some of those voices actively sought to dissuade and discredit the emerging movement, concerned that the type of direct action suggested would threaten the fragile coalitions of power they had built up within the existing framework.

Others were afraid that direct action might make matters worse and believed the community should weather the violence, focusing on the long-awaited return home. ARCAEL rejected these prohibitions and went ahead with a demonstration planned for the 12 June 1976. Beginning at the Naz Cinema, over three thousand mainly local Bengali men marched. Khosru was one of the leaders of that demonstration and recalled how there had been considerable uncertainty about whether they could galvanise the community to publicly take to the streets in this way:

> When it was the first demonstration in 1976, we went from Naz Cinema. In the beginning nobody came with me, only me and Mala and a few others – all the way to Osborne Street there was only a few people, but when we get to Osborne Street everybody come through! That's the first demonstration over the racism, the first time we came on to the streets like that – no one did it before us, not like that.

Little attention has been paid to the significance of this first march in existing historical accounts, but for Khosru and others I spoke to, this march was an essential precursor to the 1978 mobilisations in response to the racist murder of Altab Ali. Many of the younger activists involved in the vigilante patrols had pushed the elders, and in some cases defied them, to make this angry statement: there would be no retreat from the East End.

The event also illuminated the tense relationship between left parties and the Bengali community. Supportive left groups were encouraged to attend and offer solidarity, but the organisers had been clear that no organisational placards were to be brought to the march. A few accounts recall that Chris Harman of the International Socialist Group had ignored this instruction and that there was a scuffle between him and Terry. In the event no placards were carried, but Terry was not there to see that first-hand as he spent the duration of the march in a police cell as a result of the incident.

Others I interviewed were more sympathetic and open to the influence of socialist organisations. Rafique Ullah arrived in the UK as a young boy in 1972. He had vivid memories of the 1971

Demonstration organised by Anti-Racist Committee of Asians in East London (ARCAEL). Khosru Miah featured holding Mala Sen's left arm, Whitechapel Road June 1976 © Paul Trevor.

Liberation War and talked about being haunted by the violence that he witnessed. He recalled the 1978 community demonstration, organised ten days after the racist murder of Altab Ali, which managed to mobilise thousands of people in a demonstration that carried Altab Ali's coffin. He was eighteen at the time and had become involved in community organising with the Bangladesh Youth Front in response to his experiences of racism in school and the inaccessibility of youth services. He was clear that the magnitude of this 1978 'turning point' demonstration was only possible because of the earlier, locally based activities that had begun flexing the muscles of the younger generation, both in the face of the wider structures of racism and in defying the internal reservations of older, more conservative community members:

Our elders used to say: 'Calm down, we are here to just work, make some money, going back home' – that was their slogan. But on that day – when we got that message, everyone boiled! And all the youth stood up. We came out on the street and we said 'No – today, Altab Ali, tomorrow, it could be me. No more!'

Rafique Ullah thinks that there were about 12,000 people on that demonstration. He recalls taking the coffin from Brick Lane to Hyde Park and then on to Downing Street, where he was part of a small group that handed in a 'memorandum' to the police officers on the steps of Number Ten.

He also highlights that by 1978 there was a more collaborative relationship with wider anti-racist organisations:

> We never had Whatsapp, we never had mobiles, we never had messengers – nothing! But more than 10,000 people or 12,000 people came from Birmingham, Manchester, Sheffield, Leeds. Those were the industrial towns, our people used to be there, they came – by coach loads, they came. But we had not only Bangladeshi people – we had SWP – Socialist Worker Party – Anti-Nazi League support us too, they came attending our demonstration. Without their support we would not be successful.

Rafique Ullah, front centre, in a procession to commemorate the anniversary of Altab Ali's death, 4 May 1979 © Paul Trevor.

Rafique Ullah seen here in front of the Shahid Minar statue in
Altab Ali Park, October 2022 © Seema Khalique.

There are clearly mixed views about the role of wider socialist
organisations and as stated previously, some of that stemmed from
the *Race Today* position that a white working-class could not have
solidarity with a black working-class movement until there had been
considerable work around the racialised violence of capitalism and
colonialism. This was, of course, reinforced by the lived reality of
street violence that was perpetrated against Bengalis by white people
who were working class. There was also an incident where the organisers of an Anti-Nazi League carnival at Brockwell Park in 1976 were
said to have ignored warnings that a National Front attack on Brick
Lane was imminent, and many Bengali activists felt betrayed by this
failure to take seriously the threat experienced by their community.

While some of the younger activists scorned conventional political structures that didn't match their ambitions at the time, many of them did go on to become actors within those same structures in the following years. The political confidence generated by squatting and vigilantism was important; Helal and Nurul became the first Bengali local councillors in the early 1980s. For Terry Fitzpatrick, it was obvious that the housing struggle was

> ... where a lot of the younger activists cut their teeth, what they – what they were shown was: you can move into a house, you can move into a block of flats, and you can back the state off and get rehoused. So if I can do it over houses, I can do it over other things.

The squatters' movement began to gather wider momentum. Having secured a public presence by taking squats for Bengali families and gathering younger members into vigilante groups, the Bengali squatters had secured a prominence few might have imagined at the outset. With that growing power, Bengali squatters began to exert political pressure.

NOTES

1 Anne Kershen, *Strangers, Aliens and Asians: Huguenots, Jews and Bangladeshis in Spitalfields 1666-2000*, Routledge: London, 2005, p187.
2 Christopher T. Husbands, 'East End racism 1900–1980: Geographical continuities in vigilantist and extreme right-wing political behaviour', *The London Journal*, Vol. 8(1), 1982, pp3-26.
3 Shayfur Ghafur, 'Gender implications of space use in home-based work: Evidences from slums in Bangladesh', *Habitat International*, Vol. 26, 2002, p42.
4 Iftekar Ahmed, 'The rural Bangladeshi courtyard', *BRAC University Journal*, Vol. 3(1), 2006, p12.
5 This participant chose to use a pseudonym.
6 This address has been changed to protect the participant's privacy.
7 Alexander Vasudevan, *The Autonomous City: A History of Urban Squatting*, Verso: London, 2017, p55.
8 Bridget Anderson, *Us and Them?: The Dangerous Politics of Immigration Control*, Oxford University Press: Oxford, 2013, p3.

9   Colin Smith, 'Skinhead terror in Bethnal Green', *Observer*, 5 April 1970.

10 Stephen Ashe, Satnam Virdee, Laurence Brown, 'Striking back against racist violence in the East End of London, 1968–1970', *Race & Class*, 58(1), 2016, p36.

11 Ibid, p43.

12 This participant's name has been changed.

13 Ali Riaz, *Bangladesh: A Political History since Independence*, Bloomsbury Publishing, 2016.

14 Yasmin Saikia, *Women, War, and the Making of Bangladesh*, Duke University Press, 2011.

15 Nurul Hoque, *The Story of the East End Community School*, self-published, Bangladesh, 2012, p37.

16 *Credo: Blood on the Streets*, LWT, BFI archives, 1978.

17 *Race Today*, Vol. 8, Issue 4, April 1976.

18 Ibid.

19 Ibid.

20 *Race Today*, Vol. 8, Issue 6, June 1976.

21. Ibid.

22 Mala Sen quoted in Sarah Glynn, *Class, Ethnicity and Religion in the Bengali East End: A Political History*, Manchester University Press: Manchester, 2014, p126.

24 Ashe, Virdee, Brown, op cit, pp34-54.

25 Ibid

26 Glynn, op cit, pp136-7.

4

Winning tenancies:
settling down or selling out?

In my late twenties I moved to Walthamstow, East London, acquiring the E17 postcode made famous during my youth by the boy band East 17. I had both my children in my thirties in fairly quick succession, and as the blur of sleep-deprived baby days slowly moved to inducting them into primary school, I began to interact with the local community in different ways. I was a teacher at a local secondary school and despite a dual professional income and significant support with childcare from my mum, afterschool club and nursery provision were hard on our finances. I made use of the various baby and children's groups around me, the activities ranging from heart-warming to horrifying. But like many other mums – and a smattering of dads – it was the company of other adults experiencing the same early parenting rollercoaster that I sought. To begin with, I also had access to a local Sure Start Centre that offered sing-along, baby-massage and weekly coffee mornings, which were all free. I went to those and paid for other weekly sessions. By the time my son was born, most of the free sessions had been de-funded and my opportunities for interaction and respite could only be procured if I paid for them. I could manage that and did, but a whole spectrum of mothers that could not disappeared from those circuits of support. The racialised and class background of the women who stayed was middle class and mainly white. The opportunity to share experiences and have adult conversation on a regular basis provided the anchor to what were sometimes wildly unpredictable and lonely times, and yet access to that support became much more obviously rationed.

It was only during this period that I began to seriously reflect on the loneliness that my mum must have experienced when she first arrived in the UK, giving birth to me as a twenty-year-old migrant woman in a country where she had no family, friends or financial capital. During the period of motherhood where I toured baby-groups, greedy for support, my mum 'toured' various shared houses and flats, sleeping on floors, desperate to secure somewhere to settle. But sadly my mum's experience is not one that has been relegated to the archives of the 1970s.

On school runs my children had the habit of randomly making friends with other children. At the top of our road we would frequently meet the same mother and child, who was a similar age to my younger son. Our drop-off rhythms meant our children would scooter along together as we chatted. Over the period of a year I learned that her small flat above a local barber's shop was owned by a private landlord who kept changing the terms of their agreement; that he suddenly hiked up her rent as the agreement was coming to an end, and finally that she was unable to meet that demand and became homeless. Our meetings became infrequent, but when we bumped into her at the school gate now and again, we learned that she was wrangling with the council, who wanted to relocate her to temporary accommodation in Luton. Despite her resistance I found out that she eventually was moved to Luton. I saw her a few further times managing an unfathomable train and tube journey because her husband's job was based locally and they were desperate to keep it (he was the sole breadwinner). Throughout, she tried to maintain her daughter's routine, bringing her to school despite the tumult in her life, but eventually she stopped coming.

Hers was not the first or last family that 'disappeared' from our school community; there were many others who came and went, pushed and pulled by the council's housing decisions. The ability to secure one's housing, to be able to make a home in a specific location and to afford the luxury of knitting yourself into the wider fabric of the community, are still determined by council housing departments and private landlords in ways that too frequently neglect the importance of these basic human needs. In a report published by Heriot Watt University in 2022, the researchers high-lighted that Black and minoritised communities are still 3.5 times more likely to experience homelessness than their white counter-parts.[1] Whether it was my parents in the 1970s or the woman I made my school run with, the rupture of relationships based on housing deprivation and insecurity is still disproportionately experienced by racially minoritised communities.

*

'If all immigrant groups put in a similar request, it would be chaos.' This was how Tony Judge, Labour Chair of the GLC Housing Committee, dismissed early demands for tenancies and better housing from a delegation of Bengali families, accompanied by Terry Fitzpatrick of the Tower Hamlets Squatters' Union and *Race Today* activists Farrukh Dhondy and Mala Sen, in winter 1975. Gathered in front of the GLC head office at County Hall, a group of Bengali men, women and children, approximately fifty people in total, held up placards which read: 'Evict the council, not the people'; '£2000 spent on repairs and now they evict us', and 'Greater London Con-trick'. The small demonstration had gathered in response to eviction orders handed to the Bengali families that had squatted the first mass squat in Old Montague Street. The action also came after the publication of a Runnymede Trust report 'Race and Council Housing in London', which had used the 1971 census data to highlight that as a public landlord, the GLC operated gross levels of inequality in the quality of accommodation offered to tenants of 'New Commonwealth origin'.[2]

The specific demands handed in by the small delegation of Bengali squatters were:

1. All eviction notices be stayed until alternative accommodation was offered;

2. That all the families were rehoused within the E1 area;

3. That when offered alternative accommodation, sufficient notice was given so that properties could be viewed before acceptance.

In 1975 the GLC bluntly refused these demands but did concede the squatters some time, with a view to them appealing to Tower Hamlets Council to be rehoused. However, Tower Hamlets Council were no more forthcoming with their offers of housing than the GLC. Part of the problem for Bengali squatters was this bureaucratic ping-pong between the GLC and the Tower Hamlets council, the two biggest landlords in Tower Hamlets, about who had responsibility to house the Bengali families in crisis.

For many squatters, in addition to the precarious nature of their tenancy they also had to confront harassment from the London Electricity Board (LEB) and British Gas in terms of energy supplies to their home. As noted previously, squatters were legally entitled to utility supplies to their squatted homes, yet both Tower Hamlets Council and the GLC would intermittently instruct the utility companies to cut supplies, leaving families without access to electricity or heating. For Husnara this meant that she spent six months in a home heated with only paraffin heaters and had to do all her cooking outside the home:

> We used coal for heating – before you didn't have heaters, when we came there were no heaters. We used to have paraffin heaters, what choice did we have? There was no electricity – but the paraffin was so smelly – the whole house used to smell because it has such a strong smell. And candles! For six months, we used candles. Can you imagine that now?

The harassment of squatters through the constant cutting off of utility provisions came up repeatedly in my oral history interviews and archival research. In December 1976 an article in the *Race Today* journal recorded how a member of BHAG appeared at Snaresbrook Crown Court charged with theft of gas from the North Thames Gas Board. The arrest had taken place a year earlier when a police officer had caught a BHAG activist reconnecting a gas pipe to a house squatted by a Bengali family. *Race Today* reported how the gas board at the time was actively complicit with the council in harassing Bengali squatters while overlooking neighbouring white squatter families who remained connected. The Riaz family who had squatted this particular property on Essian Street had a gas meter. They had paid not only their own gas bills but had also cleared the deficit left by the previous account holder. The court heard how the family had repeatedly approached the gas board for reconnection and been ignored. On this occasion the judge summed up the case in favour of the BHAG defendant, stating that he was unconvinced that this was an act of theft as squatters were legally entitled to have gas and electricity services, and that the family in question had shown themselves to be responsible bill payers. The jury returned within ten minutes of being dismissed to deliberate, finding the defendant, not guilty.

BHAG activism was, as the episode above indicates, varied; the connection of services when they had been illegitimately denied, and even repairing properties that had been deliberately rendered uninhabitable, was a radical political act, in opposition to a council that sought to keep those properties empty on its own terms. Helal, for example, argued that BHAG brought squatted properties

> back into public ownership, many of them were ... boarded up, for disposal. Many of them mostly kept boarded up and deteriorated and therefore the value dropped. So, in a way it wasn't just about us taking over but we protected those properties, people invested whatever limited, small amount of money they had in protecting and improving the fabric of those buildings.

Terry was often the lead on the practical repair side; as a builder by trade he had the skills, contacts and access to tools. He also had a daring attitude and would often undertake risky repairs, many times at his own peril. On one occasion recalled vividly by almost everyone I spoke to, the highlight of the squatter folklore my father would tell me, Terry almost died in an explosion trying to repair a shoddy electricity cable. It was winter 1977 and Terry was trying to replace a cable that ran from a single fuse box to service the seventy-two flats in Pelham Buildings. Something went wrong and Terry was spectacularly electrocuted. Gedu, who was good friends with Terry, recalled:

> I think it was maybe three hours later, someone chased me and he said, 'Your friend is probably dead!' I run to Royal

London Hospital and they wouldn't let me see Terry because his condition was so bad. He was inside of the glass – he was really bad. I think they only allowed me after couple of days and first thing I said to him – 'you *are proper mad*, first I thought you are mad, now I realise *you are mad* – why have you done this? It's not for you or not for anybody – you could have employed someone – paid him!' But Terry, Terry, he was always there and he hasn't taken a penny from anybody. He was always a friend for the Bangladeshi people.

Terry's own recollection was that he only regained consciousness just as he heard the last rites being read to him by a priest:

I was in the London Hospital, I was in intensive care and I heard the last rites of the Roman Catholic Church being read to me, which means it's pretty much – they thought I was going to die, and I remember hearing the Latin and felt the holy water and I thought, this is serious, they think you're going to die. It was my name, Fitzpatrick, and so they thought, he must be probably a Catholic, in those days they would just assume and decide that get better get the priest in – they can't do that now, but at the time – they all thought that that was it for me …

Terry suffered severe burns and scarring as a result of the incident and was in intensive care for some weeks. He did recover and return to his flat in Pelham Buildings, where the campaign for housing continued to gather momentum. With the emergence of BHAG in spring 1976, the Bengali squatters' campaign began to develop a clearer focus. Pelham Buildings had been secured and this, along with communities of squatters in Varden Street, Nelson Street and Old Montague Street, meant that there developed something of a close network of families. This squatter community meant that they were less likely to be individually targeted by council officers and that it was easier to rally together. They started with a letter writing campaign. *Race Today* activists and those squatters like Helal Abbas who were literate started writing to local councillors requesting an opportunity to meet and discuss what they described as a housing emergency. The only response from the council was 'we don't talk to squatters', which Mala Sen pointed out was untrue since they had publicly engaged with white squatter organisations and communities and made arrangements with them based on short-term licenses and offers to rehouse. In light of this, BHAG organised a demonstration to coincide with the Health and Housing Committee meeting in June 1976.

Shafia, the young woman who squatted with her husband and stepchildren in Varden Street, recalled the drama and excitement of demonstration. She laughed as she remembered nearly being hit by a passing car when she strayed into the road, and that many of the older men had berated her for being careless and irresponsible. Eventually the demonstration grew big enough to block the road and the three hundred strong crowd sat down, refusing to allow cars to pass and demanding that council officers come out to speak to them. The demonstrators only left when the councillors allowed a small delegation to enter the building and a meeting with BHAG was agreed for August.

Mala Sen was critical to gaining the trust and attention of Bengali women; as a south Asian woman she was mindful of cultural gender norms, while at the same time since she was educated she was able to digress from these norms while retaining the Bengali community's trust. Mala would spend time conversing with female squatters and would encourage them to attend the demonstrations that were held at the town hall. For Bengali women, most of whom had been born in rural Sylheti communities where their relationships with men outside of their family and their access to 'public' political spaces was limited, attending these marches would have been a significant innovation of their prescribed social roles. Mala was attentive to these restrictions but also committed to ensuring that women were included in these demonstrations. She helped to arrange cars so concerns about safety were assuaged and so women and children would be picked up from their homes and were safely escorted back. Shafia said:

> The men, they knew that they needed us to be there, what could they do? After all, our whole argument was that we are families and we are being threatened with eviction and then

the others were saying that we are families who cannot find any house; so they needed us to be there with all the children so that the point could be seen clearly in front of their face – there is no good if they are all just men standing there. They knew that – so they let us come, but some of them still did not like it.

The demonstrations were effective: the council could not ignore the families gathered on their town hall steps and the publicity this was generating, catching not only the attention of local press but also precipitating interest from several national news outlets. Reluctantly, the council, who had thus far been entirely dismissive of the Bengali squatters, was forced to meet. In the meeting that followed in summer 1976, BHAG delegates submitted a list of demands to Tower Hamlets Council, insisting 'we had not come to beg for favours'. They claimed to broadly represent the 'interests of 35,000 Asians' who lived in the local area and for whom 'they, as elected representatives, have a responsibility'.[3]

As the first and most important priority, BHAG stated:

We are aware of widespread racial discrimination in the policies and processes for allocating housing in the borough. We demand a change in policy and an end to racism in the allocation of housing.[4]

Despite this initial meeting, Tower Hamlets Council remained firmly of the view that the council was doing everything possible to assist Bengali families who were on their waiting list. This was despite ongoing wrangling over the council's purchase of the Varden Street properties, where many Bengali squatters were living, on terms of vacant possession – that is, terms which required London Hospital to evict the Bengali squatters in order to progress the purchase. This policy seemed to be at odds with another purchase in Parfett Street, where the council had offered white squatters licenses that would permit them to stay on through another purchase.

Mala Sen, in a letter to the council at the time, noted that the council was eager to appear at an anti-racist meeting in Toynbee Hall, stating:

We believe that your appearance ... on that platform was mere opportunism. A cynical exercise in Asian vote-catching. Nothing more. You seem to distinguish between the racists who attack us on the street and those who attack us in other ways. As far as we are concerned, it is only a difference in degree.[5]

The GLC was more forthcoming in their negotiations with BHAG. They had been moved to accept, for example, that racist harassment of Bengali tenants was a growing threat to their relocation in areas where they were likely to be isolated. Tony Judge, Labour Chair of the GLC's Housing Management committees, had come under increasing pressure since the publication of the 1975 Runnymede Trust report, which had been scathing of the GLC's allocation policies. His initial dismissal that all immigrant groups would begin to flood the council with similar demands had to give way to a more moderated approach. However, even where there was some movement, for example in a pledge to establish a 'fire alarm' system whereby Bengali families who were attacked by neighbours and residents of their estates would be given priority rehousing, the council officers on the ground failed to enact its provisions.

BHAG developed its demand for a fairer housing policy overall by specifying that the Bengali community wanted to be housed in E1, the Spitalfields area. They made the case based on the numbers of Bengali migrants who worked in the local area, the schools that local children attended and the relative safety that had been accrued over time. However, this did not prevent the GLC from serving eviction notices to all the families in Pelham Buildings.

One of the critical turning points in the squatters' campaign came in May 1977, when the Conservative Party secured a victory in the GLC elections. The Tories were generally more sympathetic to the Bengali squatters. While this may seem odd, the GLC was by this stage cognisant of the fact that evicting hundreds of Bengali squatters was likely to be a costly decision, both financially and reputationally. To evict several hundred Bengali families would also add to the responsibilities of the Homeless Person's Unit and the empty houses themselves would then either be susceptible to re-squatting by another set of families or would require some form of council-led destruction, actions which, in St Agnes Place in Brixton, had led to a furore of angry publicity directed at Lambeth Council.

Jashimuddin recalled the flurry of activity after the Conservative GLC came into power:

> I may be totally wrong, this is my belief. My belief is central command on the Conservatives was beginning to see that negative publicity is not helping their cause. They had to come up with something and accept, look, this is reality, these are people who are now occupying our houses. So, if you want solutions, the solution is to declare an amnesty. House them as part of your rights and obligations of the community. Because they live in that area, they work in that area and they are paying their taxes. So you're collecting their taxes, you are helping them integrate into the British society. You allow facilities such as housing, social services, education, so on and so forth …
>
> I don't know what made them, but they actually came to Pelham Buildings, they met me. They met me and the other Bangladeshi family at the ground floor flat. Behind there is an arch entrance. It used to be an arch entrance, you go in, and in one of those rooms we hurriedly got all the chairs and things. And they came in – I talked to them, face-to-face negotiation. And I think they liked what I had put forward as a consensus on behalf of our families. We didn't have a seven-point plan, we just had one plan. And that plan is you have to promise that you will house each and every one of us. You will help us secure alternative accommodation where there is no danger to our life and living and that is within the constraints of Spitalfields.

In June 1978 the Tory-led GLC did announce a London-wide squatters' amnesty and enabled squatters to register and be allocated a GLC tenancy. For Bengali squatters, it was agreed that BHAG's key demand for housing in the E1 area would be honoured. The GLC hired the Montefiore Centre and, with a team of interpreters, set about registering the hundreds of families that were affiliated with

BHAG. Together, the GLC and BHAG established a list of local estates where Bengali families were agreeable to being rehoused.

Jean Tatham, the new Chair of the GLC's Housing Management Committee, was quoted as saying:

> There have been physical attacks on Bengalis in areas of East London away from Spitalfields and it has been suggested that they need to live as a mainly Bengali area to obtain the protection which a large group of their people can provide.[6]

A huge row developed a few weeks later when the plan to rehouse Bengali squatters in this manner was described by a GLC official as the 'setting aside of a few blocks of flats in or near Spitalfields *specifically* for the occupation of people from Bangladesh, in collaboration with the leaders of the Bengali community.'[7] This story was picked up in the national media and was covered in some detail by the *Observer*, where it became known as the 'ghetto plan'. It was reported on with headlines that read 'Squalid Tenement Blocks', 'Ghetto Estates' and 'Frightened Families'. The headlines caused much confusion – BHAG had never campaigned for segregated blocks, not least because the fear was that permitting the council to allocate 'Bengali-only blocks' was likely to replicate the existing patterns of housing allocation, which generally meant that Bengali families were offered the lowest grade accommodation. In a leaflet BHAG responded:

> We demanded that all our members be offered accommodation in 'safe areas' which we defined on a map, as sections of the E1 area ... we did not say that we wanted these estates cleared of white tenants. Nor did we say that we wanted any of these estates exclusively for our use ...[8]

The generational divergence on direct-action tactics, both in terms of squatting and wider vigilantism, were further exposed when in the same leaflet BHAG highlighted,

> It is not only the national press that has made mischief with our demands. Ironically, though there appears to be little

truth in the claim some ... self-proclaimed 'leaders' and 'representatives of the Bengali community' have also used this opportunity to attack us. They have been quick to distort our demands in their attempts to discredit our organization. They have demanded 'integration' and in effect, are supporting the old plan of dispersal. If they have their way, we will find ourselves being sent back to areas such as Poplar.[9]

As Terry said several times in his interviews, 'Poplar was like a swear word' for most Bengali migrants, and being rehoused there was unthinkable. The furore over the supposed 'ghetto plan', which was at best a misunderstanding, at worst a deliberate misrepresentation of BHAG's demands for tenancies on 'safe estates', galvanised the various communities to action. A meeting was held at the Montefiore Centre on 13 June 1978. Over 500 people attended and there would have been many more had they not closed the doors due to health and safety concerns. There were television cameras and journalists waiting to hear Jean Tatham, the Conservative Chair of Housing, speak to the gathered crowd. Local white residents saw the 'ghetto plan' as an agreement that was going to side-line and subordinate their right to social housing in the area by allocating whole estates to Bengali tenants. From the gallery, white tenants shouted 'that they were living in the dustbin of London and that the GLC was doing nothing for the white community.'[10] However, as the meeting progressed, everyone realised that in reality there was broad agreement between communities. For instance, BHAG explained that like white people in the local area, they were also not interested in segregated estates, for their part largely because they feared they would be assigned the most run-down and dilapidated estates and left there by a disinterested council. The meeting concluded with everyone apparently agreeing that the so-called 'ghetto plan' did not have community support from the local community, white or Bengali. The GLC left the meeting confused – Jean Tatham insisted there was never any plan for segregated estates. However, several of her own housing spokespeople had previously given the impression that they had intended on designating certain estates for rehousing Bengali squatters. Charlie Forman suggests it was the internal misunderstanding about the rehousing plan and the dramatic press coverage of BHAG's demands that generated such intense public consternation and anger. Indeed, in my interviews, divergent accounts of the so-called 'ghetto plan' and the 'famous' community victory over a pernicious GLC housing plan persisted, though the archival accounts reveal that it was nothing more than a straightforward concession to BHAG's demands for rehousing to 'safe' estates.

On the one hand, this was a monumental victory for BHAG. The GLC, the largest landlord in the Spitalfields and E1 area, had acquiesced to Bengali squatters' demands. A group of Bengali migrants who had individually and sporadically squatted empty dilapidated houses, and who had been exposed to the harassment of neighbours, council officials, police officers and utility providers, had used direct action to secure a commitment from the council to their rehousing. The GLC had accepted a responsibility for housing Bengali migrants whom they had previously labelled low priority, with little legitimate claim to resources. The decision to award all the Bengali families who had taken direct action and secured a squatted property for themselves a tenancy was, in this sense, an outright victory. However, there were deep reservations within the *Race Today* collective about the outcome. Darcus Howe in particular was worried that the rehousing of Bengali tenants was a hollow victory – that securing tenancies for the members would dissolve the broader political aims of BHAG. By late summer these tensions spilled over and a scathing editorial signalled the end of *Race Today*'s support for BHAG:

> As far as *Race Today* Collective was concerned, the organisation had to devote its energies to the consolidation of its membership, through a clear statement of policy, a paid-up membership and a structure which would reflect the organisation's stance against the state on housing. Such a membership, subscribing to a political organisation, could not see themselves simply as beneficiaries of any deals which an executive committee made on their behalf with the state agencies. Neither could they see themselves as receivers of low grade accommodation, which the organisation could provide by perfecting the tactics of squatting.[11]

Darcus Howe berated BHAG for drawing up the lists of safe estates and registering its members for the amnesty. They had, as far as he was concerned, acquiesced too easily and allowed the GLC to hollow out the movement by accepting meagre concessions. He continued: 'It will give BHAG members tenancies in vacancies on derelict estates, and in this way, whittle away its membership'.[12]

Of course, in many ways Darcus was right – the strength of BHAG dissipated once Pelham Building squatters were rehoused and the sense of collective power and struggle was neutralised. But this comes back to the differing ambitions of those involved in BHAG. Jashimuddin and his family were rehoused to one of the newer estates. He recalled, 'my wife thought that this was the best thing she had since coming to London, that she could secure the front door and have a bath'. For them, the attractions of the Pelham Building community could not compete with the joy of having a decent flat, with all the 'modern' conveniences of a bathroom and hot water, and a secure tenancy in a mixed estate.

It took a little longer for BHAG members in surrounding streets to have their housing situation resolved, but there was a slow dissolution there too. All those who I interviewed from Varden Street were awarded tenancies in the houses they had occupied or rehoused if the accommodation was considered unsuitable.

As Terry remembers:

> It took a long time for the Bangladeshi tenants to get rent books because that was Tower Hamlets. It took a while for Varden Street and Nelson Street squatters to be rehoused, but there were no evictions. And the important thing to remember is that 2,000 Bangladeshis occupied state-owned properties and there was not one single eviction because the government, the state, whether it was Labour or whether it was Conservative, were frightened of the consequences.

The Bengali squatters in Pelham Buildings may well have been 'bought off' by being awarded tenancies, but most of them squatted because they were deprived of adequate social housing. They took the opportunity that presented itself in the housing landscape that existed at the time and decided to occupy the empty properties that were left by both the GLC and Tower Hamlets Council. They were aware of the racialised dimensions of their housing deprivation – this reality was inescapable given that it was not only the state neglect of their housing needs but the street violence that made living in isolated pockets of Tower Hamlets so existentially threatening. While there was significant crossover with *Race Today*'s political objectives, the alliance was one of mutual convenience rather than necessarily a case of shared objectives.

Race Today wanted to champion community self-organisation and direct action by migrant groups in Britain as a key part of their political agenda. The Bengali squatters needed the support of activists who could provide the practical, legal and organisational support to help them develop into a focused movement. The Bengali community were resisting state and street racism, but the terms by which they defined success was their ability to win tenancies – being rehoused out of Pelham Buildings or being awarded tenancies in their squatted properties *was* the victory. Though it might have been seen as selling out or settling by *Race Today*'s agenda, being offered council tenancies was the core objective of squatting for most of the Bengali community who participated in BHAG. Most were working hard to earn an income for survival here and to be able to send remittances back to *Desh*.

Mala Sen, who was closer to the community through her regular activism, seemed to understand this:

> We did change people's minds, we did make them feel ... a more kind of ... community sense rather than an individual sense, yes. We made strides. I don't regret that movement, I think we achieved a lot, but I think we had a limited agenda. I mean, you can't create a world revolution with ghetto politics ... and it was ghetto politics ... After that some of us felt we'd done what we had to do and we had no more to say. They were taking over their own lives and good luck, that's what we wanted them to do anyway, and we moved on to other things.[13]

Following the GLC amnesty, many squatter groups across London shifted into cooperative housing models. In their 1970s guise this meant that groups were given funding grants and were able to purchase and allocate housing according to rules and criteria decided by the governing body, in cooperation with their tenants. Many Bengali squatters were attracted to this model, which seemed to offer some direct control over their housing aspirations. Charlie Forman, who arrived in Tower Hamlets during this period, was particularly impressed with how many of the Bengali squatters grasped this opportunity and used the power to develop housing that suited the needs of the Bengali community, in contrast to their previous experiences. Many of the 'big brother' type squatters who I interviewed, like Luqman Uddin, Khosru Miah and Helal Abbas Uddin, progressed out of the squatter movement into the more formalised structures of housing cooperatives. The Sylhet Housing Co-op, for example, was formed by a group of Bengali squatters who bought thirty-four houses in Parfett Street from Tower Hamlets Council. There were others too, including the Shajalal and Mitali Housing Co-ops, which enabled Bengali families to shift from being squatters into joining co-ops that were controlled and run by the Bengali community. The portfolio of properties was not always well thought out and many were in poor condition, such that the funds required to repair and make them habitable were beyond the pale. Many of these infant cooperatives struggled to find their feet in the 1980s and into the 1990s. Some of them failed to survive that period and were bought out by bigger housing associations. *Race Today* might have felt vindicated by these outcomes, which seem to suggest that the institutions and structures themselves would inevitably fail to meet the needs of the Bengali community. But many Bengali squatters felt an incredible sense of pride that, within the space of a few years, they were able to purchase significant housing portfolios from a council that had until only recently deprived them of social housing.

Helal Abbas, who had arrived in 1968 as an eleven-year-old boy; who had talked about a 'successful day' at school being defined by his ability to avoid being beaten up by racists, moved from being secretary of BHAG to secretary of the newly formed Spitalfields Housing Cooperative. He recalls with considerable pride that the housing cooperative was able to deliver housing for not just the Bangladeshi community but others too. Helal went on to be elected as a Labour councillor in 1985. Like Nurul Hoque, a

Pelham Building squatter and co-founder of the East End squatted community school, Helal found that the local Labour Party at the time was not especially warm to nominating Bengali candidates to its lists. Hoque failed in his first attempt at selection and went on to stand as an independent in the 1982 council elections. He won, unseating a safe-seat Labour councillor. Helal was clear that the primary reason that the Party selected him by the mid 1980s was because they realised that the electoral numbers in Tower Hamlets were beginning to stack against them:

> The host community did not see a reason to embrace the migrant community – migrant was a dirty word … the host community only reacted when they saw a threat or benefit. So when Nurul Hoque defeated a sitting Labour councillor – a safe seat – they had to take notice. By the 1980s the Labour Party had begun to realise that unless they took us in, they would lose seats to us. So it was mutual benefit rather than mutual respect that changed things. And Bengalis thought, if we can get a seat around the table – why not?

Helal was one of those who did go on to take a seat around that table – he spent twenty years as a Labour Party councillor and was leader of the council for another five years after that. Having spent his childhood years escaping racist bullying, he went on to gain his educational qualifications through attending night school and studying at weekends. He recalled with pride that he spent a large part of his local political career advocating for better educational provision in the borough. For him, one of the signs that the Bengali community had turned a corner in their migration and settlement journey was that towards the end of his time as councillor his weekly surgeries, once dominated by residents queuing to get forms filled and letters read because they were unable to read and write English, changed character and began dealing with traditional constituency concerns. This, Helal noted, was because 'we put a graduate in every family'.

Helal has three adult children now. His older brother, who he squatted with in the early 1970s, has since moved out of Tower Hamlets. He has, as Helal describes it, a 'lovely big house in

Redbridge'. Helal smiles as he registers the difference between them. Helal's brother finds Helal's attachment to Tower Hamlets both as a home and as a place for continued political and community-based work difficult to fathom. Though not explicit, the sense is that once Helal's brother had an option about whether to stay in Tower Hamlets or to move out, he decided upon the latter with little hesitation. Helal distinguishes between those who took 'flight' from Tower Hamlets and those like him who stayed. He describes it as though he had little choice – for him, the slogan 'here to stay, here to fight' defined not just the struggles of the 1970s but his ongoing commitment to social justice for Tower Hamlets communities.

Others of that 'big brother' generation also stayed and continued with their activism beyond the expiry of BHAG. Soyful, who had arrived in London in 1977 and squatted in Nelson and Parfett Street with his family, was involved with Luqman Uddin in the setting up and management of the Sylhet Housing Cooperative, which sought not just to acquire and distribute property but to design the redevelopment based on the specific housing needs of Bengali families. This meant ensuring, for instance, that there were enough bedrooms for the traditionally larger Bengali family, and the installation of extractor fans in the kitchen so that cooking smells were adequately dispersed. Charlie Forman was employed in housing advice services through the Spitalfields Housing and Planning Rights Service (SHPRS) during this period. He recalled that the architects employed in these new housing cooperatives were invited to speak with Bengali women in focus-group style discussions so that they were able to influence how the refurbishment of older properties was managed. Charlie remembered that Bengali women were very clear that they wanted open-plan style arrangements in their living area reminiscent of the rural *bari*, where room spaces are less defined by doors and flow into each other. Soyful was also appointed vice-chair of the GLC's Housing Action Area, which targeted funding in the 1980s into redeveloping properties in the area. Both Soyful and Luqman were further involved in community organisations in the local area including St Mary's Community Centre, which helped to support wider community initiatives such as the campaigns to name several new primary schools after key Bengali cultural and political figures, like the Kobi Nazrul School in Whitechapel.

Soyful Alom in Altab Ali Park, October 2022 © Seema Khalique.

The East End Community School, which began life in a squatted basement flat of Brunswick Buildings in Goulston Street in June 1977, was in many ways the seed for these later campaigns around the importance of cultural inclusion and representation in mainstream education. Nurul Hoque and his wife, both Pelham Building squatters, started the school as an effort to preserve Bengali cultural autonomy in a mainstream schooling system that was discriminatory and alienating for Bengali children. The school started as a self-funded and community-organised initiative and was initially subject to hostile council interactions, including eviction threats and closing orders. Beginning with a small donation of books and chalk from Avenues Unlimited, a local youth project, it secured a small funding grant from the Spitalfields Project and after eighteen months secured further funding from the Bethnal Green Institute of Adult Education. By 1979 the squatted school was given portakabin accommodation in the nearby Davis Mansions Playground. However, in the early 1980s as part of GLC redevelopment of this area, the school's accommodation again came under threat. In a letter of support Caroline Adams, then a youth and community worker in Tower Hamlets, wrote about the school's evolving position and its fight for survival against a hostile local council:

> As the school's reputation grew, the scandal of its overcrowded condition became known to the local authorities who devoted ... more effort to attempting to evict the school. One of the teachers was twice taken to court in the attempts to close the school. The committee, however, held firm to their determination that the school would not close until suitable alternative independent premises were provided.[14]

She went on to state:

> For children and parents alike, the school has been a focus, which has given them, as nothing else in their life in Britain has given, a sense of belonging and significance.[15]

She also noted the wider role the EECS played in inspiring similar supplementary schools across the borough. One of the key characteristics of the school's approach to negotiations was its insistence on autonomy:

> It has been suggested that the school can be housed in the premises of some of other institution rather than having its own premises. This is a suggestion that the Management Committee have always firmly resisted, even when the school seemed most endangered because the essence of the school is that it is the community's own institution, a tangible power base and pressure base within an oppressive society.[16]

The school was eventually given a new site on Old Castle Street, only a short distance from where it had started life as a squatted basement school. By the mid 1980s the EECS was integrated into the Inner London Education Authority (ILEA) supplementary schooling strategy, but neither the EECS nor other such schools fared well in the decades that followed as a consequence of shifting political priorities and the funding cuts that came with them.

Khosru continued to squat for some years after the dissolution of BHAG and only left his squatted flat when he was given a housing cooperative tenancy as part of his new job as a caretaker for the Spitalfields Housing Cooperative. He went on to work in many different jobs, including in an insurance company, catering and taxi services. He was injured in an accident several years ago, which impacted on both his memory and mobility, and he has since retired from all work. He lives with his wife and two daughters on the border of Hackney and Tower Hamlets. While at the beginning of our interviews he had been adamant that he could never leave the East End, more recently his desire to be near his married son and his grandchildren in Chadwell Heath meant that he had agreed to sell the council flat he bought through the 'right to buy' scheme in order to buy a house closer to them. This decision, though a departure from his original position, was not surprising – every conversation I had with Khosru was littered with stories about his grandchildren. Like many of the older participants, he was regretful of having worked so hard when his own children were younger. Grandparenting offered a luxury that he had been ill able to afford in the 1980s and 1990s. Khosru had visited Bangladesh regularly until recently and would spend a few months at a time there whenever he visited. But he recalled that his most recent visit after his brother-in-law's death had been short. He had not been able to settle and did not even go to visit his natal village *bari* before returning to London. Bangladesh no longer gave him the comfort that it once had – home was now dictated by his familial attachments to East London.

Gedu did not squat. He stayed in his rented property, but in the mid 1980s when he went 'home' to Bangladesh, got married and returned with his family, he began to experience his own housing hardship. His account is a reminder that though the early housing crisis peaked and dissipated with the Bengali squatters' movement in the mid 1970s, Bengali families continued to experience evolving forms of institutional discrimination into the 1980s and beyond. In the 1980s and 1990s initiatives like the revived Sons and Daughters scheme recycled ideas about indigeneity as a prioritising factor for council housing.[17] Gedu described the hardship of those years and how, eventually, the family were awarded a council tenancy. He went on to buy a small maisonette with a garden near

Hanbury Street, but he explained that his children became unhappier as they grew older and dreamed of moving away from the East End to a bigger house with more space. The family moved out to Essex, but Gedu's dissatisfaction with this local migration was inescapable – he described himself as drawn like a magnet to Brick Lane and that he felt terrible anxiety if he had to stay away for too long:

> Home? Home is Brick Lane – Hanbury Street. I love living in Hanbury Street. If I get an opportunity now – I'll come back to Hanbury Street. Because I have lived in Hanbury Street all my life. I've met so many people – I've done so many things. Hanbury Street is my home.

Terry and Gedu remained friends. Terry went on his first (but not last) trip to Sylhet as a special guest at Gedu's wedding in 1985 and continues to remain tightly connected to the local Bengali community. Terry's position within the movement was challenging; he had no interest Black Power politics and indeed was deeply cynical of the *Race Today* collective's involvement. However, he was committed to the rights of the Bengali community to access social housing and considered it unreasonable that they were treated so poorly. He was also very clear that the Bengali squatters' movement was critical to the more well-known anti-racist movements that developed in response to the 1978 murder of Altab Ali. Being a white man in a Bengali community movement seems to have caused him little difficulty. In many ways he was more critical than Bengali interviewees of the way he felt leftist organisations had tried to co-opt the Bengali community struggle and use it as a recruiting ground. In Terry's eyes, these organisations only paid lip-service to the racialised experience of the Bengali community. He described one episode shortly after the media furore about the so-called Ghetto Plan where the Anti-Nazi League (ANL) organised an anti-racist carnival at Brockwell Park. Along with Bengali activists, he said that they had information from local white families that the National Front were going to use the opportunity to launch an attack on Brick Lane. The carnival organisers failed to listen and there were only a handful of local Bengali young men that stayed locally to defend Brick Lane and faced the wrath of a National Front smashing spree:

> What happened then was the Anti-Nazi league had their rally in Brockwell park in South London and we knew what was gonna happen because I was getting fed information from white families, there was going to be an attack and we were saying look, we need several hundred people to be around Brick Lane, but they were not interested. In the end people got bashed over the head. I got punched in the nose, Abdul got his windows smashed. There was – there were about two to three hundred NF that ran down Brick Lane, 200-300 people – there were about 30,000 at Brockwell Park.

Of course there are alternative accounts of these events, and the ANL were critical players in anti-racist organising during this period, but for Terry and others this episode reinforced their belief in self-reliance and that the broader ecosystem of institutions, including those on the left like the Labour Party and ANL, simply did not understand the needs of the Bengali community. Terry continues to live in East London and remains close to local political developments, where not dissimilar conversations around whose interests are served by current Bengali leaders in positions of power, and others who court Bengali political loyalty, continue to play out.

For all the 'big brother' types, their housing journeys after squatting or squatter activism affected what tenancies they were awarded and, in the subsequent decades, what discussions they had with their own children about whether or not to stay in Tower Hamlets. The older, 'uncle' types, who had arrived with a view to returning 'home' to Sylhet, had to navigate the more complex, transnationally embedded loyalties in their housing journeys. For migrant men like my father, Masabbir, the enduring commitment to the transnational family they had left in *Desh* consumed their energy. Masabbir's remittances have, for fifty-seven years, supported his wider *gusthi* (extended family) and *attiyo* (distant family relation) with housing, utility line extensions, business ventures, migration opportunities for brothers and nephews, purchase of agricultural land, medical expenses, weddings, burials, and pilgrimage trips to Mecca.

Abdul Masabbir (my dad) outside our *bari* in Chattak, Sylhet,
in December 2022. Personal photograph.

In the early days of his migration, Masabbir tells me he was absolutely committed to 'returning home', and imagined his large family living in the house he built with many years of remittance money. He moved his mother and youngest brother into the *basha* (town house) he was building. He made sure that they had all the home accessories that you would expect in a *Londoni basha*, including air conditioning, fridge-freezers and satellite televisions – facilities that he would never enjoy himself, except as an occasional visitor. In contrast to the remittance home they built in Sylhet, Guljahan, his wife, recalled how frugally they lived as migrants in London, always with their heads and hearts focused on the return home.

It was only in 1988 that the couple, exhausted by fighting a council that refused to give them anything bigger than a 2.5 bedroom flat, finally put down a deposit on a four-bedroom house in Hackney. Ironically, the postcolonial immigration system had, through its inflexibility, created the conditions whereby a family that had been disinclined to make a more permanent homemaking decision felt they had to choose one location over the other. Masabbir lamented the years of hard work and the frugal life he had lived in order to save for this return home:

And I am retired now, but before I was thinking I would retire there permanently. Nowadays my plans have changed. I have seven children, I have fourteen grandchildren, and if I go there and settle down there and sleep and get the rent, that's not what will make me happy ... I want to be near my children, I want to be near my grandsons and granddaughters. That is the situation. But it was a very, very hard life to build all this up ... My mum is dead, my dad is dead, only one brother and two sisters in Bangladesh now. So I'm going for a visit soon, but I don't know how long I will stay. I think of all that money I invested and the way I worked to send that money – it's really – it makes me want to cry when I think of it! And if I kept that money here, and bought some flat or some ... house or anything – maybe I would be more happy? But still, on the other hand I'm happy because I'm going soon for a holiday and I have a place in town and I have a place in the *bari*. Alhamdulillah – yes, with that I am happy.

There is an ambivalence in what Masabbir describes here – the reference to 'all that money I invested' should not be underestimated. Like all my interviewees, Masabbir worked in the lowest paid jobs in an economy that was willing to exploit his labour, but which denied him and his family entitlement to state resources like secure housing. It would be easy to pin Masabbir's choices to his hopes for a romanticised return to Bangladesh, but that would overlook the global economic inequalities which lead people to migrate to the UK in the first place. It also would not account for the racialised immigration laws which restrict freedom of movement for migrants, preventing people like Masabbir from living a more transnational life in the first place. Masabbir's sadness over the years of toiling in restaurant kitchens, which were invested into building a remittance home he now knows he will never inhabit, was a familiar story.

Guljahan, my mother, was not just a 'family reunification' migrant – the term often used to describe migrant women who travelled to join their husbands in London in the 1970s and 1980s – she was also an economic migrant in her own right, who remitted to support both her husband's family and her own through her home garment work. In addition to this often invisiblised economic role, she also worked to ensure that her children were culturally trained for a transition back to Bangladesh, a home she retained a close connection to through remittances, gift-giving, regular communication and the cultural home life she nurtured. All her children were taught both Bengali and Arabic, and all seven of her children have retained at least a basic level of Bengali literacy into adulthood. I first interviewed her the day before she was leaving for an extended visit to Bangladesh. She was still busy with last-minute packing, having already sent a large parcel of family gifts as cargo. She was reluctantly going to assist with the legal work around their remittance investments. She had never returned to Bangladesh without at least some of her children and she was anxious about staying away, even though we were all adults and no longer lived at home. In this way she was similar to the Bengali elders in Katy Gardner's ethnographic, narrative-based study in Tower Hamlets, who worried about failing health and access to medical care, and who no longer achieved a sense of comfort from returning to the place they had once intended to be their permanent home.[18] When asked about her feelings for the remittance house where she would be staying during her visit, Guljahan was unambiguous: 'It is my number two home. Because this is the first one – this is where my children grew up, this is where they all are – they all are here.'

Guljahan had originally wanted to return home in the early 1980s because she was concerned about the corrosion of traditional cultural values. She remembers worrying about her daughters' propriety in a culture that did not conform to the norms of 1970s rural Sylhet. But despite this worry, she remembers that the dissatisfaction with their council flat and their inability to secure a home for their growing family led to the balance beginning to tip in favour of finding more suitable settled accommodation in London. In the mid 1980s when her oldest daughter was starting secondary school, the couple began to actively discuss whether to buy a house here or to make the agreed move back to Sylhet. Guljahan said:

> Yes, we wanted at that time to move back. Your dad said that my children are getting bigger, they were all old now and he wanted to take everyone to *Desh* and he wanted you to be schooled in Bangladesh, he didn't want to stay here, it was

not important to stay here. I said no, I didn't want my children to go to Bangladesh, because I thought they can't do their education there or here, they won't finish anywhere. So I never went, and I never went for visits without you – it's the first time I'm going without you now.

Guljahan's account adds nuance to the idea of 'double belonging'; both of my parents expressed that while they retain commitments and attachment to *Desh*, their home is unambiguously located with their children and grandchildren in London.

Guljahan Begum (my mum) in her home in Hackney,
October 2022 © Seema Khalique.

Sufia also talked about her homemaking ambitions as revolving around her concerns as a mother. She and Abdul Kadir had squatted twice, and it was from their second squatted flat in Spitalfields that they finally secured a rent book. Kadir had not only squatted himself but also supported the growing group of squatters that came to occupy the estate where he lived. He advocated on behalf of his neighbours, securing housing advice and legal support to help them both resist eviction and campaign for legal rights. When he finally did secure a tenancy for himself, he made sure that all his Bengali neighbours in the estate were offered the same agreement. When speaking to him about these activities and events, his description of them was always perfunctory – he simply did not have any choice but to stand up for himself and those around him. To him it was a question of survival. As far as he was concerned, he hadn't come all the way to London to be deprived of the right to a decent home. Getting a tenancy after years of housing hardship was the beginning of the family's housing journey through and beyond the Tower Hamlets social housing system. The couple themselves remain council tenants in a flat in Tower Hamlets, while their children are scattered around East London. Like my parents, for Sufia it was her commitment to her children's education which was the deciding factor in the late 1980s for giving up on the dream of a return home. She realised that they had invested too many years in London and could not go back to mainstream education in Bangladesh without her children suffering a detrimental impact. She said: 'My home is here, I am at home here, in this country. For me, I am at home here – here is where my children are – it's where I get peace, yes. I don't really want to go back.'

Sufia asserts clearly that her sense of home is based not around the houses that they sent remittances to develop and maintain in Bangladesh, but rather was anchored in the UK by her children and her grandchildren. She says quite categorically, 'Why would I go back?' The home imaginary that had directed so much of their early remittance practices and had captured their affective loyalties was now an empty *bari*. Sufia and Kadir now live in a council flat in an area that would have provoked horror in them in the 1970s because of the level of violence that isolated Bengali families suffered there. Now that home is, in many ways, the heart of their extended, multi-generational family, full of photos of their children and grandchildren, birthday bunting permanently looped across one wall in celebration of the many grandchildren's birthdays they enjoy together.

Husnara is the only squatter who has remained in the property that she squatted over forty-five years ago. After the wrangling between the London Hospital and Tower Hamlets Council about the sale of squatted properties requiring vacant possession, eventually all the squatters were awarded a tenancy with Tower Hamlets Council. Since that time Husnara has spent only two years living outside of that property when, in the mid 1980s, she and all other social housing tenants were temporarily rehoused while their homes were refurbished. She recalled that they had been offered the opportunity to be rehoused permanently when the redevelopment started. While others had accepted this, she insisted on moving back when the work was completed. She remembers that for the opening event in 1988, after the completion of the redevelopment, her family had been approached to hold an 'open house' style event for the local press and council officials who were marking the occasion. She remembers how she made hundreds of samosas and hosted the event outside her house, with people visiting inside to see the outcome of the two-year redevelopment project. Now her English garden is set up with trellises that are thick with Bangla *khodu* plants and bear *khodus* of generous proportions. When asked about where she was most happy and at home, she responds:

> I'm happy here [London], yes. Happy because – where I have my *shekur* (roots) – my *shekur* is Bangladesh, but my branches and leaves are here, they have grown here. My branches and leaves – my children are my branches and leaves, so I think my branches and leaves need to stay here – I understand that – but still I love my *Desh* – my Bangladesh, I love it.

Her use of roots and branches as a metaphor for the way her family has evolved and how that impacts on her 'need to stay here' may be a familiar one, but it is nonetheless a powerful testimony to her extraordinary journey and her attachment to her once squatted

Husnara in her back garden, October 2022 © Seema Khalique.

home in East London. Husnara managed to retain her social housing tenancy after the redevelopment of her street. That has certainly not been the case for many Bengali families in present-day Tower Hamlets. Much of the Bengali community who now remain in Tower Hamlets have experienced a staggering volume of 'redevelopment' in their area. The associated gentrification that has accompanied it has, for many, become the most active and persistent threat to the community's place in the East End today.

NOTES

1 Glen Bramley, Suzanne Fitzpatrick, Jill McIntyre, and Sarah Johnsen, *Homelessness Amongst Black and Minoritised Ethnic Communities in the UK: A Statistical Report on the State of the Nation*, I-Sphere, Heriot Watt University and Oak Foundation, 2022.
2 Runnymede Trust, *Race and Council Housing in London*, Runnymede Trust: London, 1975.
3 *Race Today*, September 1976, p184.
4 Ibid.
5 Mala Sen, 'What is racism? The Bengali experience in the East End', *Race Today*, May 1977, pp66-7.

6 Charlie Forman, *Spitalfields: A Battle for Land*, Hilary Shipman: London, 1989, p84.

7 Ibid.

8 Bengali Housing Action Group, *Asians and Housing*, June 1978. A5 leaflet, Institute of Race Relations.

9 Ibid.

10 Ibid, p202.

11 *Race Today*, July 1978, pp109-110.

12 Ibid, p110.

13 Sarah Glynn, *Class, Ethnicity and Religion in the Bengali East End*, Manchester Press: Manchester, 2014, p137.

14 Letter written by Caroline Adams in the records of the East End Community School, Tower Hamlets Local History Library and Archives, 1983.

15. Ibid.

16 Ibid.

17 The 'Sons and Daughters policy' was brought in by the Liberals (later Liberal Democrats) in the mid 1980s and was designed to give preferential access to council housing to sons and daughters of existing tenants. This in effect gave lower priority to homelessness, which was generally higher in the Bengali community, and higher priority to the sons and daughters of white families with existing tenancies.

18 Katy Gardner, *Age, Narrative and Migration: The Life Course and Life Histories of Bengali Elders in London*, Berg: Oxford, 2002.

5

'Tower Hamlets is not a place
you live forever'

My parents left Spitalfields and Tower Hamlets in 1976 and have not returned to live there since. My family experience of Tower Hamlets after we left was gendered. My dad would go regularly, as our family groceries and remittance business was conducted there. The East London Mosque and Brick Lane Masjid were both anchors for him, and to some extent my brothers. As an adult I returned mostly to the Sunday market and the new Spitalfields Market, realising that I was now part of the new middle-class purse that these redevelopments were seeking to attract. But it was only starting my PhD at Queen Mary University of London, based in Mile End, which brought me back to Tower Hamlets properly.

In preparation for my first year I visited Tower Hamlets Local History Library and Archives. I found myself standing moments from Mile End Hospital, the place where my mother had given birth to me as a young migrant woman, knowing little English and without a single family member or friend to rely on. Later, I went on to conduct part of my fieldwork by setting up a regular weekly visit to local community centres where I would drink tea, play bingo and watch Bangla TV with Bengali elders. In so many of those conversations, the elders would often remark that they had never talked to their own children about these experiences – that they had either been too busy or not interested in recounting these experiences.

On reflection, there was probably also a mixture of shame and trauma in that reticence. There were some who I spoke to who felt that digging into our squatter history did not reflect our community in a way that was appealing or powerful. Others felt there was a level of shame that I risked exposing in discussing the poverty-stricken conditions that Bengali migrants had first experienced when they arrived, which they no longer wished to be reminded of, or indeed associated with. I think for others there was unwanted trauma in revisiting that period – to step back to a time of acute physical and material vulnerability was not an easy thing to do.

With my parents, because we spent so much time together having these discussions, there were moments when all of these different sentiments came up – shame and trauma, but also joy. There were tearful moments too as we picked over difficult periods of their lives. My dad described to me a house fire that had killed two young migrant men in one of the shared accommodations he had stayed in before my mum arrived. The men, both new arrivals, had jumped out of top floor windows to escape a fire started by a faulty paraffin heater. I managed to track down a newspaper article that reported the events and shared it with him – both of us cried in that conversation. Despite those tears, my parents were gratified that I was interested in exploring and marking their history. We even went back to 12 Deal Street together and talked about how the life they had imagined behind those broken windows and damp walls was so far removed from where they ended up nearly fifty years later.

I am one of their seven children. Between us, we are a mixed bag of mainly public sector professionals, with traditional and non-traditional family set-ups (my parents have had to adjust their measurement of 'success' to accept our cultural divergences). On the other hand, now that my siblings and I are older, we are attentive to the hardships they endured and the sacrifices they made on our behalf, in order to give us different choices and opportunities. As parents ourselves, we all fret about how our children – second-generation British Bengalis – know and interact with their heritage.

Even as both of my children have observed my research journey, I recognise that their Bengali identity is significantly – and predictably – different to mine. There is a pronounced disconnect for them; they speak little Bengali, and so conversation with my parents is sadly limited. At the same time, through this work they have been connected to a rich and powerful history, one that weaves them into struggles that have defined the British polity. They understand the phrase 'we are here because you were there' in a way that I did not until I was an adult. They have inherited a very different relationship to Bangladesh and their Bengali identity to my own, but they also understand the complex tapestry of connections between the histories of Britain and Bangladesh in a way that I was not given the opportunity to develop until much later.

*

Tower Hamlets continues to be home to the largest concentration of Bangladeshi people in the UK. Many of the people I interviewed remain in Tower Hamlets, though many have moved further eastwards in recent decades into Barking and Dagenham, Ilford and Redbridge. Some suggested that they chose to move. However, they universally related those 'choices' to the type of accommodation that was available to them in Tower Hamlets. The contemporary struggles that Bengali communities encounter are not dissimilar to those of the 1970s, albeit in a significantly changed political landscape. While in the 1970s the 'un-homing' experience for Bengali people in East London was connected to overt state and street racism, in 2022 there is a sense that racism operates in subtle and invisibilised ways; that it is baked into the system in a way that makes it almost undetectable, except for the pronounced racialised outcomes it delivers.

In 2021 early census data revealed that Tower Hamlets is the most densely populated of London's thirty-three local authorities, with around 112 people living on each football pitch-sized area of land compared to an average of three people across England.[1] The borough also has the third highest unemployment rate in London, as well as high levels of deprivation and child poverty. The child poverty rate is the highest of all London boroughs, with a recent study by Trust for London indicating that 56 per cent of children in Tower Hamlets are living in poverty compared to a London average of 37 per cent.[2] In terms of housing need, the council and other Registered Providers operating in the borough have more than 20,000 households on the housing waiting list, and there are a further 9,500 households classified as 'overcrowded'.[3]

The poverty, overcrowding and homelessness reported by the council in its demographic analysis are not evenly shared across communities. The 2021 Census data released showed that Tower Hamlets is the most densely populated London borough. The more detailed demographic analysis is yet to be released, but in 2015/2016 it was found that 80 per cent of households accepted as homeless were from minority ethnic groups, and that 'Asian households' are more likely to be overcrowded and homeless than any other ethnic groups in the borough.[4] One estate that has been making regional news headlines with its campaign against housing association landlord Tower Hamlets Community Housing (THCH) is Charles Dickens House, Bethnal Green. Justice for Tower Hamlets Community Housing Residents have been campaigning for months to get their landlord to take action on the poor condition of many of the flats. Residents have reported living with leaks, damp, mould and pest infestations that hark back to the conditions Charlie Forman described in flats occupied by overcrowded Bengali families in the 1970s. The death of two-year-old Awaab Ishak in November 2022 due to mould in his parents' flat highlights how fatal these issues continue to be.[5]

During the Covid-19 pandemic, overcrowding played a clear role in the disproportionate number of deaths experienced by the Bangladeshi community in Tower Hamlets, with the council reporting that Bengali people were almost twice as likely to die of Covid as white British residents.[6] In a report for the Runnymede Trust, James Nazroo and Laia Becares concluded that the health inequalities exposed by Covid-19 were a consequence of 'persistent racism'. They highlighted that 'living in overcrowded housing is an important risk factor for Covid-19 infection because it may not permit people to socially distance or to self-isolate if needed'.[7] They went on to state:

It's difficult to justify a disproportionate focus on biological and genetic explanations for higher risks to COVID-19. There is no one gene for being black or being Asian. Race is a social construct. More likely than having a shared genetic or biolog-ical predisposition is that some ethnic minority groups live in disinvested neighbourhoods with high levels of pollution and concentrated poverty, with insecure and underpaid employment, and in overcrowded conditions with substandard levels of housing; that these socioeconomic, housing and environmental factors are shaped by institutional and structural racism; and that discrimination is deeply embedded in the daily lives of people from these groups.[8]

Even in the latter stages of the pandemic, Bangladeshi communities continued to experience higher death rates than their white counterparts.[9]

In summer 2022 when the Conservative government's Covid-19 inquiry was being set up, the original terms of reference omitted any specific questions about the unequal health impacts on minority ethnic communities. Following significant cross-party and civil society pressure, the government widened the remit to include some scope for that line of inquiry. While that investigation is ongoing, another creeping, persistent pressure has been undermining the community's sense of belonging in Tower Hamlets. Some of the housing gains won by Bengali squatters have since been jeopardised not by the racialised housing deprivation inflicted by the local councils, or the brutal violence that terrorised the community in the 1970s, but by the process of gentrification.

THE VIOLENCE OF UN-HOMING

Ruth Glass coined the term gentrification in the 1960s to describe the pattern of middle-class people who had moved out to the suburbs returning to areas of the city that had been the reserve of working-class communities. In the process, working-class communities were being displaced by both the cost of rent or property prices more generally. Adam Elliot-Cooper et al, in a paper called 'Moving beyond Marcuse: Gentrification, displacement and the violence of un-homing,[10] add that this displacement is not due to increased land and property values alone, but also because of a wider rupture with the local environment. The comforts of shops and services which made the neighbourhood feel 'homely', which nourished the community, are slowly replaced by those that service the new group. In this sense a community is effectively 'un-homed' while still living in the area. For many in the Bengali community who I spoke to, 'affordability' was often cited as the reason for recent migration patterns further east, but also this sense that the local area was moving away from them. Much of the affordability issues and changes in local services are connected to development and regeneration plans that have shaped the borough in the last few decades.

In her book *Edge of Empire: Postcolonialism and the City*, Jane Jacobs wrote a comparative study of three cities, including a study of London that closely explores postcolonial struggles in Spitalfields.[11] Jacobs locates some of the early seeds of gentrification in the formation and work of the Spitalfields Historic Building Trust in 1976. This organisation came into being with a mission 'to preserve buildings of architectural or historical importance' and was made up of architectural historians and conservationists.[12] The group used their funding to purchase and restore mainly Georgian buildings in the local area, which they believed to be under threat. Jacobs describes their methods of acquisition and conservation as a 'form of guerilla activism with business acumen'.[13] In the early days some members of the Trust squatted properties that were threatened with demolition, but more generally they used their purchasing power and accessed preferential low interest loans to purchase Georgian properties, encouraging, at the same time, a specific group of sympathetic conservationists to do the same. In order to ensure aesthetic and cultural compliance, the Trust established strict guidance about the repair and restoration of the properties, with an agreed set of tradespeople employed under the supervision of specific architects. Jacobs notes that the demographic of this newly emerging community, though not all English, were generally white European.[14]

Even in the 1980s there was some local opposition to the Spitalfield Trust's mission. These voices expressed concern that the restoration of the Georgian houses to private dwellings had displaced Bengali-based garment manufacturing workshops. By the late 1980s, properties that had been selling for between

£3,500 and £15,000 were already reaching heights of £500,000. The Trust was sympathetic to these concerns and made sure to include provision for Victorian industrial buildings where these workshops might be relocated to within its portfolio of property interest. Yet there remained an uneasy tension between the Trust and the Bengali community given that they were also loudly opposed to the damage and deterioration caused by Bengali workshop practices on these 'fine but fragile historic' buildings.[15] Charlie Forman, who worked for the Spitalfields Housing and Planning Rights Service (SHPRS) during the 1980s and wrote the book *Spitalfields: A Battle for Land* (1989), argues that the behaviour of the Trust had a long-term displacing impact on the Bengali community:

> In the process, the people who lived and worked there had been turned out, and a new Spitalfields middle class had been born. Yet it was the Bengalis who were the true heirs to the buildings – they would have been the people able to keep the houses in the mixed use for which they were built, with both living and workshop space.[16]

Charlie alludes to the fact that Bengali squatters were in their own way major contributors to the conservation of properties that may well have otherwise been demolished. Helal Abbas, for instance, recognised that Bengali squatters occupied some of the most dilapidated properties and invested both money and care into restoring and making those properties habitable:

> We were living in houses white people didn't want to live in – they left. They were appalling, they were dilapidated, they were rundown. I think one of the things was we bought those houses into use, back into public ownership.

This highlights how, in the same way that the Bengali squatter movement has had its wider social and political impact diminished until now, the Bengali community's role in 'heritage' and 'conservation' has also been overlooked. It is commonly agreed that the white squatters of Spitalfields were employing 'sophisticated methods' when they squatted two properties already in the process of demolition and attracted 'front-page publicity by scaring off the wrecking crew … throwing a dinner party in the street outside, complete with candelabra and caviar'.[17] Contrast this to the 'insufferable labour' that was needed to restore dilapidated properties to a standard fit for habitation, labour that has been rendered invisible in discourse on conservation of the area, disavowing the value of everyday actions performed by hundreds of Bengali female squatters in their efforts to make a home.

The small-scale, 'gentle antagonism' between the Spitalfields Trust and the Bengali community in its protection of a limited number of Georgian properties is dwarfed by what Jacobs and others describe as the 'mega developments' of the later 1980s.[18] Initiated by Thatcher's deregulation of the markets and the liberalisation of planning controls that prompted the City's finance sector to reach outside of its ancient boundaries, Tower Hamlets began to experience some of the largest and most expansive redevelopment schemes in London. Charlie Forman describes the battle for land that began in the 1980s as 'the most uneven fight, between Britain's poorest and most recently settled residents and some of the world's most powerful institutions.'[19]

One of the major projects begun under the auspices of redevelopment of the area was the relocation of the Spitalfields Wholesale Fruit and Vegetable Market, a project awarded to the Spitalfields Development Group (SDG). The new plans for Spitalfields Market saw the extension of City-oriented planning ideas into the previously protected Spitalfields area, as the local council saw potential for significant private investment. Jacobs follows the interaction between this new mega-development plan and the Spitalfields Trust. Initially, the Trust was supportive of the idea, and even saw potential benefits since the proposal suggested further relocating Bengali garment workshops out of mixed-use Georgian properties into more 'appropriate' locations. None of these exchanges were explicitly racialised – Jane Jacobs described it not as an overt 'geography of rejection', but as a form of 'managed multicultural cohabitation'.[20] She argues that while the Spitalfields Trust was conscientious in managing its public relationship with its Bengali neighbours, and maintained friendly dialogue with the community, their position was based 'upon a multiculturalism of convenience which provided a place (a discrete space) for Bengalis so that there might be more room for the elaboration of English heritage.'[21]

The SDG group in charge of the Spitalfields Market development likewise highlighted their commitment to the local community and to ensuring that their plans were attentive to the aesthetic and cultural heritage of the area. There were specific commitments made for 'planning gains' to be percolated into the local communities, with dedicated streams of funding. However, in the 1990s as the development progressed and various architectural designs were presented to planning committees, the Spitalfields Trust came out in opposition to the development. They argued that the ideas felt Americanised and were incongruent with the conservation needs of the area.

With the closure of the Truman Brewery in the late 1980s, another development began stirring local aspirations and anxieties. The Truman Brewery complex on Brick Lane had its bottling plant adjacent to Pelham Buildings. Pelham Buildings was demolished in 1980 after the last squatters were decanted. By 1989 the brewery too had stopped operating, and the twenty-seven acre-site came up for redevelopment. A new development scheme was launched and, mindful of the protracted negotiations of the Spitalfields Market project, the developers were quick to launch the Spitalfields Community Development Group (SCDG) to facilitate local consultation. Following consultation with local communities, they pledged to give over a portion of land for social housing, workshops, retail units and community facilities. A second key commitment was the creation of a 'Banglatown', a cultural destination showcasing Bengali cultural life, including shops, restaurants and cultural venues. In the early discussions housing was included in the mix of uses for the new Banglatown. It was argued that '[t]he presence of family and children will enhance the vitality and the authenticity of the whole area' – Banglatown needed a Bengali community for it to be a viable and authentic place.[22]

The development of Banglatown as a distinct cultural centre for the Bangladeshi community may have seemed an impossibility to the Bengali migrants who had been squeezed into overcrowded accommodation and confronted the brutal violence of the National

Front in the 1970s. However, by the 1990s a small coalition of local Bengali restaurateurs and community activists had pushed this commitment on to the agenda and were now actively campaigning for the Banglatown dream. Tower Hamlets Council, in partnership with these local businesses and other third sector organisations, put together a proposal to access funds from 'City Challenge', a regeneration funding scheme. The bid was successful, securing £7.5 million a year for five years. This, along with other funding initiatives, recouped a total of £42 million for the area's redevelopment.

However, there was consternation about the proposal from many within the Bengali community, who claimed that the Bengali restaurateurs who were active within the CDG were marketing an 'essentialised' version of Bengali culture in order to promote their own commercial interests. Helal Abbas, who had gone from Nelson Street squatter to BHAG secretary, was by now a local councillor, and called the plans 'naive and opportunistic', claiming that those involved in the project were far from representative of the wider community. His worry was that Brick Lane was being marketed for an external audience without any real reference to the needs of the local community in terms of housing, training and jobs.

Helal Abbas referenced the redevelopment of Canary Wharf, an area that had seen decades of divestment. He looked at what happened with these initiatives and argued that:

> If you go to Canary Wharf – yes, there are Bangladeshi people working in them, but a lot of them are working as admin assistants, door supervisors, office juniors – how many of them are trained managers? I think those are the jobs that we need to prepare for and aspire to. We need to break those barriers for our children ... Why shouldn't our children aspire to live in those luxury apartments? But they are not going to do it unless the local authority facilitates that through training programmes, through planning powers, but also by ... developing partnerships with employers, because they need people to run those companies. Those companies will not survive unless they can be persuaded to train a local workforce that reflects the community – that will be loyal. They will remain longer ...

Helal was pointing out inequalities that remain true today: educational improvements that had been secured in the borough were not translating quickly enough into better jobs or employment prospects for local Bengali young people.

Nevertheless, the narrative of community benefit prevailed. Key to the redevelopment scheme was a plan to invest in Whitechapel Art Gallery and Rich Mix, a community arts hub, to act as cultural destinations and support the diversification of the local economy. Brick Lane was to anchor the concept with its curry houses, but the promise was to enhance the community's cultural mark on the space. However, what was delivered was a much-diminished version of the promise, with only limited aesthetic concession to the more holistic potential of 'Banglatown'. In 1997 Tower Hamlets officially renamed the southern end of Brick Lane 'Banglatown'. The Banglatown development brought ornate gateways to the street and painted streetlamps, and grants were made available for local business owners to improve their kerbside appeal by upgrading their facades. The 'Banglatown brand' became a marketing tool and new annual street festivals were launched on Brick Lane, including an event to celebrate the Bengali new year, Boishakhi Mela, and a new Curry Festival. Furthering the 'curry capital' theme, in 1999 the borough's planning office authorised the conversion of a series of retail units in the central section of Brick Lane into restaurants, designating the area a 'Restaurant Zone'. Brick Lane was ostensibly transformed from a street that witnessed regular and brutal 'paki-bashing' sprees in the 1970s into an area where the Bengali community were centred for their historic local ties and culinary contributions.

While the Banglatown development may not have delivered on the cultural heritage promise of early plans, the history of anti-racist struggle was marked in some measure in 1998 by the renaming of St Mary's Park, close to where Altab Ali was murdered, in his name. The renaming was not without opposition. Luqman Uddin squatted in Fieldgate Mansions and is still a tenant in the same area over forty-five years later. He recalled how, as a member of the local tenant's association, and in his voluntary role at St Mary's Centre, he and other local activists had begun the campaign to get the park renamed Altab Ali Park in the 1980s. He was seventeen at the time of the murder and had been in London less than two years. He remembered clearly hearing the news of Ali's death and the grief and rage that energised the demonstration which followed.

The campaign began at a time when the Liberal Party in alliance with the Social Democratic Party had taken control of what was previously a Labour council stronghold in Tower Hamlets. The alliance came to power without openly advocating anti-immigrant policies. However, their strategy of dividing up the borough into seven discrete neighbourhoods was seen as a way to prevent Bengali people from asserting majority control in any of these new neighbourhoods. During this period Luqman recalls how hard it was for the activists who were campaigning to memorialise the community's anti-racist struggle and wider heritage:

> You know the Altab Ali Park name, well in 1986 or 1985 – then as a local resident I represented the tenants' association to the local council – that, how can we remember the name of Altab Ali? We wanted a memorial and we put in that we would offer 50 per cent of the cost in St Mary's Park for a steel arch, but officially nothing was done. So we joined the Labour Party then – I'm still a member and I was in the CLP, that's how it started. And the arch is still there, and St Mary's Centre gave 50 per cent and local council, Tower Hamlets, gave 50 per cent. But in the 1990s the council became Liberal, and they didn't want the name Altab Ali Park, and so in 1993 when the Labour came back to power – and again it's me in the committee – and you know that Mayor John Biggs – he was there – we again raised it and we wanted the names reinstated and so after we again reinstated those names and Altab Ali Park again reinstated with the council.

Luqman's account attests to the importance of public memorialisation as part of the Bengali community's affirmation of its place in the East End. He went on to talk about other campaigns, including the renaming of a local school as Kobi Nazrul Primary school. During the period of Liberal Party control over the council, it was directed to revert to the original name, Settles Street School, before finally coming back to the name that the local community had previously nominated and campaigned for.

Claire Alexander is Professor of Sociology at Manchester University and has followed the place-making practices of the Bengali community in East London through and beyond these events. In one of her articles, 'Contested memories: The Shahid Minar and the struggle for diasporic space', she begins by describing an *Ekushe* event in Altab Ali Park in 2008, ten years after it had secured its new name.[23] *Ekushe* (which means twenty-first in Bengali) is a commemoration of the date that five students were shot dead in Dhaka by Pakistani police in a crackdown on Bengali language demonstrators in February 1952, now known as Bangladeshi Language Martyrs' Day. The Shaheed Minar is the 'Martyrs' Monument' erected in Dhaka near the site of those deaths and a smaller replica of this monument now stands in the south-west corner of Altab Ali Park. In Tower Hamlets this monument has become an opportunity to mark the intertwined histories of the long struggle for autonomy and cultural recognition in Pakistan and the anti-racist struggles of 1970s London. The replica of the Shaheed Minar was the result of a local and international community campaign and is symbolic of the powerful transnational component of Bengali diasporic identity in Britain. The monument also speaks to the connection that the Bengali community has to Tower Hamlets and how closely that attachment is situated in memories of struggle and resistance, both here and in Bangladesh.

Alexander picks out the *Ekushe* celebration because she argues it helps to explore 'some of the ways in which ideas of ethnic community and cultural identity are created and performed as part of a process of memorialisation, and the ways in which this memorialization (and by extension, the "community") is itself contested in the shifting time and place of multicultural London.'[24] Professor Alexander's work is important because it offers a rich view of Bengali communities in East London, highlighting in particular the religious and secular tensions that have accompanied discussions about identity and belonging within the community over the last two decades. In her article, she also reviews the importance of the liberation struggle in Bangladesh, tracing its relationship to local anti-racist struggles:

The Shahid Minar in Tower Hamlets is a smaller version of this original monument, and likewise symbolizes a mother with her fallen sons, backed by the red rising sun resonant of the Bangladeshi national flag, and encapsulating both national beginnings and national sacrifice – the blood of the Language Martyrs. As such the memorial concretizes an emotional, historic and imaginative link to Bangladesh's liberation struggle, and to the nation that emerged from it … At the same time, the Shahid Minar and Ekushe in Tower Hamlets constitute sites of struggle and contestation, inclusion and exclusion, narration and silence, which tell a more complex story around the Bangladeshi community in the UK, and in East London, about the struggle for recognition and belonging and which open up demotic and discordant local, national (British and Bangladeshi) and diasporic stories.[25]

Both the renaming of Altab Ali Park and the Shaheed Minar statue inside it were won through local community campaigns, sometimes in opposition to the prevailing politics of the local council in the 1990s. The Banglatown concept and some of these 'memorialisation' practices were considered, in many ways, a coming of age for a Bengali community who was asserting its identity and interests in a place where they had once faced attack. However, in practice Banglatown continued to prove problematic, with many arguing that it remained superficial and traded on culinary habits developed to appeal to the English palate, representing nothing more than the commodification of Bengali 'culture' for marketing purposes.

Jane Jacobs' work explores how local left-wing groups navigated some of these developments, arguing that they positioned themselves as paternalistic protectors of a 'marginalised Bengali community', and were confounded when the Bengali community refused this narrative:

There is, for example, a notable measure of Bengali business entrepreneurialism and some powerful sections of the Bengali community are active participants in the new-style, market-linked, community development initiatives which became a growing feature of Spitalfields under Thatcherism. This predominantly male, small business sector is politically powerful and the local Bengali institutions it has established and the community development alliances it has formed, directly challenged the Left's traditional hold over the political destiny of Spitalfields.[26]

Jacobs goes on to argue that these local Bengali businessmen were critical to the development of the Banglatown concept; they were not helpless victims in the conversation but deliberately traded on essentialised versions of their culture to influence the development process in a way that might benefit their local economic ambitions. Far from being unwillingly exploited, this was a powerful group who believed that Banglatown could increase their profits, establish opportunities for local Bengali youth to benefit from new employment opportunities, and generate wider community benefits. Jacobs concludes that the interests of the different voices within campaigns to either support, moderate or oppose the development plans produced their 'own spaces of exclusion' and 'processes of displacement', and speaks to the complex range of positions within the community.[27]

The Old Truman Brewery complex did not feature as part of that early Banglatown project because in 1995 it was bought in a private sale for £4 million by the Zeloof Partnership, a family-run business with a long relationship to the East End garment industry. With the sale, the site could no longer feature in the council's broader redevelopment plans. It was privately redeveloped into the current complex, which hosts hundreds of small, independent businesses, retail outlets, cafes and bars. These developments attracted a renewed footfall to Brick Lane and the establishment of the Vibe Bar in the complex boosted the night-time economy.

Despite some misgivings, this early phase seemed to deliver on the promise of economic regeneration. Many of the older Bengali garment workers had already shifted into restaurant work due to a decline in the retail trade, as a result of competition from nearby Green Street in Newham. Banglatown's stamp as the 'curry capital' was thus, for many, a welcome marketing strategy. In a report for the Runnymede Trust, 'Beyond Banglatown: Continuity, change and new urban economies in Brick Lane', Alexander et al conclude that the 'development prompted a boom in the number of Bengali-owned "Indian" restaurants. By 2003, there were 46 such establishments, and at its peak, the number of "Indian" restaurants on and around the southern end of Brick Lane reached over 60'.[28]

In another paper called 'The rise and fall of Brick Lane's "Curry Capital"', Sean Carey outlines how initially

> Brick Lane's curry restaurants prospered, with a customer base comprised of five main groups: City workers; digital creative and fintech operatives; domestic and international tourists; students; and hipsters in search of 'cool'. The last group was composed of white British and European middle-class kinship-lite young people who proactively sought the grittiness and authenticity of the poly-ethnic inner-city experience available in and around Brick Lane.[29]

However, even at its peak there were voices cautioning that the 'curry capital economy' was reaching a point of saturation. Carey interviewed Shiraj Haque, who owned multiple restaurants on Brick Lane, and who warned that focusing on the 'curry theme' jeopardised the vibrancy of the area and limited the growth of other cultural commerce. In some senses the diversification of the local economy did happen, but it happened further north of Brick Lane in Shoreditch and in the new Spitalfields Market, which began to attract new, street-food style outlets and a range of restaurants.

The last decade has witnessed the decline of Brick Lane as the 'curry capital'. Carey concludes that there were many interrelated factors which contributed to this demise, including the geographical shift for what became more neo-bohemian bars and clubs towards Shoreditch, which had fewer trading-hour restrictions. One clear sign was when Vibe Bar, which had been widely attributed with attracting a new customer base for the 'curry capital' market, shut down in 2014, claiming stricter licensing laws had made trade untenable. There were also changes in public transport with the reconstitution of Shoreditch High Street Station, which created a new gateway to the area away from Whitechapel and Aldgate East at the southern entrance to Brick Lane, shifting footfall to the north. Carey also notes a more general shift away from a culture of the 'big lunch', which undermined the lunchtime trade that had been the heart of the traditional 'Indian' restaurant economy.

Alexander and Carey also observe the shift in the type of *retail* activity in the area, and how this has impacted on demography:

> Along Brick Lane, a niche economy has come to the fore, supported by high 'footfall' and a strong presence of tourism, as well as a markedly changing demographic. Many of the niche stores are oriented to either the visitor or a changing demographic that includes an expanding student population as well as middle-class consumers.[30]

Alexander and Carey argue that the trend is

> exemplified by the chocolatier Dark Sugars, which has two outlets on Brick Lane, and grew from an experimental market stall in nearby Spitalfields Market. Dark Sugars opened its first shop in 2013, at the northern end of Brick Lane, and a second in 2015, on the site of the former, iconic, Clifton restaurant. Chocolates are both manufactured and sold on the street, with a single small bite priced at around £1.[31]

The shift is felt by people like Abdul Kadir, who squatted in the 1970s only a short distance from where these changes are now evolving:

> Yesterday I went to Whitechapel and I went around Brick Lane – I haven't been in a long time – and I saw a lot of shops closed. Lots of restaurants gone, a few travel agencies – gone, closed. Taj – a grocery store – it is very old, it wasn't on Brick Lane first, it was first in Hunton Street. The boys who run it – they know me – they were like, '*Sasaji* [uncle] – what are you up to?' I asked, 'What's the matter – why's your shop not busy?' And they said, '*Sasaji* – it doesn't get busy like it used to because people have moved on'. I said, 'What's the issue?' They said, 'The issue is rents and rates – people can't stay here anymore because the rents and rates are too high – so people

are leaving – they can't afford it'. So in one word, people will leave, they are already leaving – they are going other places.

Taj Stores was founded by Abdul Jabbar, a seaman who came to Spitalfields in 1934. Jabbar settled in the area and opened the first store in 1936. His brother, Abdul Khalique, joined him in 1952 and the pair worked together, growing the business and moving to Brick Lane in 1956. They moved several more times before settling to where the shop is currently located at 112 Brick Lane. From the beginning Taj Stores served the local Bengali community and was also one of the main suppliers to the local restaurant trade. However, as recounted by Abdul Kadir, there is a growing sense of doom about the prospects for the store. The custom the shop enjoyed was based on both the restaurant trade and local Bengali community, so both the business and the residential shifts have affected their viability. Carey outlines how these broader shifts in the area have changed the ethnic and class mix of the area:

> … Many hipsters rented rooms in flats on the Chicksand Estate that had previously been occupied by working-class Bangladeshi families. Many of these families had acquired ownership through the 'Right to Buy' scheme but later sold their properties to Bangladeshi property developers (often successful Brick Lane restaurateurs) and moved east to Newham, Redbridge or Barking and Dagenham to secure larger housing units.[32]

The 'hipsterfication' of the East End has been well reported. Phil Hubbard, in the article 'Hipsters on Our High Streets: Consuming the Gentrification Frontier', explores the complex business and residential shifts that have seen the arrival of a new type of affluent consumer and resident in Tower Hamlets, and asks 'are hipsters entrepreneurial urban pioneers or exploitative parasites? Or both?'[33] He warns that, despite carefully crafted markers that seem to align this group with working-class communities – for instance, their anti-corporate and localised consumption values – 'we would do well to remember that the ironic consumption of working class culture, the kitsch and the retro is not something that is affordable to all. "Poor chic" does not involve the simple purchase of, and display, of second hand or discount goods. It requires serious disposable income to clean and restore such goods, turning the merely shabby into "shabby chic".[34]

There is, of course, an impact on housing too. Julie Begum, a community activist and co-founder of the Swadhinata Trust, a Bengali heritage community group, outlined what she argued were gains that had been made since the 1970s. Her parents arrived in the 1960s and went on to secure a housing association property. Julie highlighted that the kind of overtly racialised discrimination of the 1970s, and later the more insidious discriminatory alloca-tion practices like the 'Sons and Daughters policy' in the 1980s, were no longer acceptable in modern day Tower Hamlets. She also expressed some optimism that the council was making efforts to build new social housing in the borough, a move she welcomed:

> I'm heartened by the fact that councils are allowed to build new housing … there are blocks of flats going up and they are for local people to live in. So it's not as grim as it used to be – but there's still a long way to go to make housing more equitable.

Julie was cautious in her positivity, recognising multiple and inter-locking problems that still needed attention. Some of these problems were exacerbated by the process of gentrification. People like Jalal had experienced considerable housing hardship as a young migrant and finally secured a tenancy in the late 1970s. Decades on and many moves later, he used the right-to-buy scheme to purchase his council property, which he then sold to generate capital to purchase a house in Redbridge. He lamented that he 'couldn't afford to live in Tower Hamlets'. Jalal expressed discomfort with the fact that his actions contributed to what Adam Elliott-Cooper et al have identified as one of the key drivers of gentrification, where council residents purchase their properties and sell on, often to private landlords who then rent them out at 'rates typically far higher than council rates in neighbouring homes'.[35] Jalal said that the purchase was 'against my principles', acknowledging that the right-to-buy programme has been responsible for the wide-scale, slow erosion of social housing stock in Tower Hamlets. For others, like Julie, the 'right-to-buy' issue is more complex:

> I understand that these are often people on a low income, families who are just trying to live a decent life and they're often not just doing it for themselves but they're doing it for their families – here and overseas – there's lots of things going on … I'm not a supporter of right-to-buy, never would I want social housing to be … for people to buy it all up. However, I understand the need for people to be able to have a better quality of life, to generate a bit of income for themselves and not to live in such poverty as well, so it's complicated.

When he was fifteen, Mashuk's family had used squatting as a strategy to secure the fifty-two-week stay needed in order to qualify for social housing. His father had lived and worked in the East End for more than a decade before the family arrived in 1973, but the trip home to help his family move had cost him the continuous residency qualification. The family had squatted several times in the 1970s and Mashuk was still squatting into the 1980s before he was given a council tenancy in Stepney. Mashuk stayed in this flat for twenty-five years before using the right-to-buy scheme to buy it, moving to Grays in Essex. Mashuk was deeply regretful of the move. The house they had bought was much bigger and they had a private garden, but he said 'I didn't feel nothing good there … it was lonely. If you have a big house and no people with you, it's lonely … big garden – big rooms, but lonely.' Mashuk argued that this pattern of people moving out of the area meant that the community presence was likely to 'disappear, only old people stay there now – the young people move out – they want bigger houses and a garden … they win that and lose their community'. The family moved a few more times before settling in Manor Park, East London, where they traded the bigger Grays property for a smaller house, with as much proximity to Tower Hamlets as they could now afford. As Mashuk observed, 'Once you move out, it's impossible to come back in'.

Others, like Khosru Miah, also bought their council houses. Up until the time of my interviews he had resisted the push out of Tower Hamlets. However, in the pattern noted by Mashuk, Khosru's eldest son and his young family had moved to Chadwell Heath – perhaps, like others, paying the price for right-to-buy through reduced access to social housing. Now he, too, was considering selling the property he had bought through the right-to-buy scheme and joining his son there so that he could maintain something of the extended family network of care and support that is integral to Bengali familial structures. For Khosru and others, what state and street racism had been unable to accomplish in the 1970s was now, some fifty years later, being achieved by a new set of housing conditions that made it virtually impossible for residents on an average income to stay in Tower Hamlets.

Khosru also related a sense of disappointment and disillusionment with how the community in Tower Hamlets had fared. As a father of four children, he spoke about the drugs and violence that had punctuated their experience of the area and how 'we report it to the police –but nothing happens – it is there – right on the corner of my estate – but no one does anything. It's because they don't care.' In my conversations with young people in the borough, many also echoed the sense that Tower Hamlets was not an attractive place to live, and they too hoped to move out of the borough to 'bigger houses' in 'less crowded' areas.

After the conclusion of my PhD, I offered a series of workshops about my research in Tower Hamlets schools. In one Year Nine geography lesson a pupil spoke of 'the noise and the pollution – all day long – all you hear is the noise of police cars and their sirens. I want to live somewhere where it is peaceful – not here – it's just noisy and dirty here'. Another girl in the same class talked about drug dealing on her estate and how she imagined escaping 'the congestion – I want to live somewhere where there is space.' When asked whether a bigger house in Tower Hamlets could entice her to stay, she bluntly stated that the big, nice houses were for the 'white people – not people like us.' The same was said about the new developments of flats that were going up in and around their communities. In a Year Twelve class, one pupil spoke about the feeling that these new builds were not for Black and brown communities, and that no one she knew could afford the rents in these new buildings.

The impact of reduced social housing and a private rental market that caters to new, middle-class workers was epitomised in one Year 12 student's account of her own family's housing journey. She recalled how her parents, who migrated from Italy to London in 2016, had initially rented a three-bedroom flat on the Isle of Dogs. While there, the landlord decided to raise their rent, giving the family one month's notice. They were unable to afford the rent rise and she recalled her parents trying desperately to find a new place to live, made harder by the fact that her mother was heavily pregnant. Unable to secure a similar sized three-bedroom house, the family had to move days after her mother had given birth into a much smaller property where, like 1970s Bengali migrants, they had to use the living room as a bedroom. Another student described eleven members of her extended, multi-generational family living in a two-bedroom flat, waiting on the council to re-house them. They felt that there was almost a perverse reliance by the council on the fact that, if things got bad enough, the family would sort the issue for themselves by dispersing and moving out.

Since the Covid-19 pandemic, Sean Carey and Claire Alexander have returned to their 'Beyond Banglatown' interviewees to review how traders have fared. In their report 'Revisiting Brick Lane: Impact of Covid-19', the assessment is pessimistic. They report that curry house owners believe Bengali Brick Lane to be in danger of disappearing, in the same way that Jewish Brick Lane has. They reported that trade was running at 10-30 per cent of expected turn-over for those that had managed to reopen, while others had simply closed all together.[36]

While some comparison can be made with the previous Jewish and indeed other East End migrant communities, it is important to note that these other communities generally moved out of the area as they became more affluent, to places where the quality of housing and the space available was superior.[37] Conversely, the existing Bengali community is being pushed out because the *East End has become too affluent for them*, due to a lack of social housing, the unaffordability of privately rented accommodation, the neglect of the state in managing their neighbourhoods and the dwindling of amenities that cater to their needs.

One of the most recent developments to have galvanised the

community is the proposal to redevelop the Old Truman Brewery complex into a new shopping mall, offices, restaurant units and outdoor terraced dining facilities. The proposal has created divisions within the community between those who see it as an opportunity to resuscitate a dying Brick Lane and those who believe it is the final nail in the coffin for the area and must be resisted. The final section of this book picks up on how younger Bengali activists have begun to mobilise against the proposal and how some older community leaders and activists have challenged that resistance as misguided.

SAVE BRICK LANE?

In the conversations surrounding the more recent campaign against the development of the Truman Brewery site, it is possible to detect a shift in how Bengali community history is being mobilised. In particular, this new generation of community activists has begun to reach into the 1970s housing struggles and squatters' movement as inspiration for their campaign. Traditionally, it was the anti-racist mobilisations of 1978, following the death of Altab Ali, which assumed priority over the contribution of earlier Bengali squatter activists to the community's history. Helal Abbas who, like many others, agreed that the squatters' movement was the birthing ground for the wider activism that developed in 1978, thought that while squatting was the issue around which the community became organised and began to exercise their direct-action muscle, it had previously been a quieter history:

> Squatting was not going to be the platform for popular community organising – we come from a fairly conservative background ... breaking into places – really, dilapidated properties – for lots of people – this was putting the reputation of our community at risk, so it was not going to be the marketing face for our community mobilising.

Perhaps the community's own disinclination to foreground squatter histories and the wider narrative that housing-deprived migrant squatters were politically uninteresting were together responsible for the erasure of the Bengali squatters' movement in academic research and writing. But in recent years, and with the Save Brick Lane campaign, there has been something of a renaissance in the way that younger activists have begun to reassess the role and importance of the 1970s housing struggle, and to consider how it might speak to the more recent struggles around gentrification. In 2020, at the height of the Covid-19 pandemic, the owners of the Truman Brewery put in a proposal to develop the site into a complex of offices, shops, restaurants and a gym. The reaction to the development has been mixed and the spectrum of responses in many ways has polarised local communities. On one end, there has been public outcry at what is seen as the latest and most intense gentrification offensive, signalling the end for the remaining vestiges of local community life along Brick Lane. At the other end is the hope that some moderated version of the development might resuscitate ailing local business. There are of course others who sit somewhere in the middle, as reflected by people like Julie Begum, who feel that the noise generated by these heated debates drowns out the more everyday concerns of local people:

> … most people I know who live and work in Brick Lane couldn't care less about these campaigns – we're getting on with our lives, we've got other things to think about – more important things to think about. We're really not interested in a car park being developed or not. I can't get cross about that. There are other things that are more important to me.

That said, there are people within the community who are anxious about the proposals and for whom these debates directly impact on their ability to be and feel at home in Tower Hamlets. The Zeloof Partnership who own the site issued what they hoped was a reassuring statement, outlining that the new complex would create several hundred jobs for local people. They reported that the architectural designs were sympathetically drawn so that the new site would suit the aesthetic character of the area and did not involve demolishing heritage buildings. They also set out that the benefits drawn to the area would be shared by the local communities. However, from the outset many in the local area felt that the development had little interest in the community where it will be situated. For Saif Osmani, founder of Bengali East End Heritage Society,

> [w]hat was really shocking, was, if you look at the computer-generated images, none of them have Asian people in them, or Bengali people in them. Like, you monitor that? I've worked for developers, for a short period, temporarily. And they would always discuss that, who is it for? Is it accurate? Is it pushing too far? The fact that they didn't, is actually saying that the northern end of Brick Lane, isn't for you.

Claire Alexander and Sean Carey similarly concluded that the 'Truman Brewery development ... is likely to significantly alter Banglatown's unique historical, social and cultural significance as well as Brick Lane's "Indian" restaurant sector.' They recommended that the local council should 'work with local communities, schools and heritage societies to actively protect Brick Lane's conservation status as part of recognising the unique position of the lane in the history of migration and anti-racist struggles.'[38]

The conversation with the council that they suggest has not been an easy one – many in the opposing campaign argue that the council has been reckless and negligent in the way that it has surrendered community interests to glossy redevelopment plans. Fatima Rajina is one of the co-founders of Nijjor Manush – a phrase that means 'our own people' in Bengali – an organisation which describes itself as an 'independent campaigning group that aims to educate, empower and organise Bengalis and Bangladeshis in the UK'.[39] Fatima, though not originally from Tower Hamlets, came to have a close connection to the area as part of her doctoral and post-doctoral academic career. Nijjor Manush have been one of the leading voices in the Save Brick Lane coalition, which was set up in response to the redevelopment proposal. The group was formed in 2018 by likeminded individuals who felt there was a need for an organisation that nurtured Bengali cultural heritage, but framed this within a political discourse of power:

> ... culture is political and the cultural entails politics ... but we just didn't want to be known as that – just that we get

together, wear sarees and jam with friends – what we do is
political.

Nijjor Manush shaped its identity and objectives in the thoroughly
modern space of a WhatsApp group, and began to organise events
that promoted the political value of celebrating Bengali cultural
heritage. For example, they designed the *Fora* programme, which
revisits the radical histories of south Asian and Black Power organising. It was during the first lockdown in spring 2020 that Fatima
was approached by a local councillor about the Truman Brewery
proposal, and was invited to bring Nijjor Manush into early discussions around a local coalition to oppose the development. Fatima
described the introduction to the other interest groups, which
included the Spitalfields Trust and the East End Preservation
Society, thus:

> Initially it was those two organisations that were involved.
> And then we had few meetings with them. I think all of us
> were very cautious of one another in our meetings because we
> didn't know who anyone was other than common denomi-
> nator, which was [the local councillor] basically. And then
> after those meetings, we would all give each other feedback
> like, what did you think of this? What did you think of that?
> And then, we were happy to go ahead and discuss strategising
> around the next steps.

Almost all the activists involved in Nijjor Manush are from academic
and professional backgrounds – some are the direct product of
what Helal Abbas described as the educational revolution that was
the product of 1990s Bengali campaigning and local educational
reform. On their website, Nijjor Manush offer a simple reasoning
for their rejection of the proposal:

> Spitalfields has suffered a tsunami of soulless corporate devel-
> opment spreading from the City of London, inflicting ugly
> steel and glass blocks at odds with the narrow streets of old
> brick buildings here.
> In spite of local protests, the City of London has success-

fully used its power to impose land grabs, expanding its financial industries into Tower Hamlets.[40]

The ability to navigate the planning application process and the broad coalition that they were able to develop has been important to how the campaign was able to gain traction. Fatima explained:

> We split into a few little groups making sure that at least one person Bangali speaker in each group, and we split north and south end of Brick Lane. And that day, I kid you not, we knocked on every single business that was in Brick Lane. And we managed to get ninety businesses to object to the proposals.

The campaign used a range of different activities. In one particular event, another Nijjor Manush activist described how they chose the railway bridge that had once marked the line between the part of Brick Lane that was relatively safe for Bengalis and the part that was dominated by the National Front for a publicity stunt to announce the campaign's slogan, 'Save Brick Lane'.

> The first thing we decided to do was a banner drop ... Now in order to do the banner drop – it was going to be on the railroad bridge, which meant climbing whole thing, and myself and a few others ... I don't know how we did it looking back. And we did it in Yiddish as well. So we put the banners up, and because the banner was so heavy it just took us ages. And then we went to the other side, northern end, we dropped it in Yiddish and English. The southern end we dropped it in Bangla and English.

The initial volume of objections to the proposal meant that the planning committee deferred their decision and the coalition again set about organising to speak with residents in all the neighbouring estates. By this stage, other local organisations had joined the coalition, including the House of Annetta, a newly opened social centre in Princelet Street, an area which was formerly part of the Bengali squatted terrain. House of Annetta was able to provide a meeting space for the developing coalition and Fatima recalls sitting in their cold meeting space once lockdown measures were relaxed. Pooling their resources to create campaign materials – both physical flyers and social media posts – the campaign began to secure national and international attention, getting hundreds of thousands of likes and shares online.

The campaign continued for months, with volunteers collecting thousands of signatures while talking to local people about the implications of the development. They went on to organise rallies ahead of the planning committee vote. Invoking the 1978 demonstration where Altab Ali's coffin was carried through East London, the demonstrators silently marched down Brick Lane holding a coffin marking the impending death of Brick Lane should the proposal go ahead. Their campaign's sophisticated social media presence is indicative of the younger profile of the activists, yet they have also actively cultivated links with historical struggles like the Bengali squatters' movement of the 1970s. Sotez Chowdhury, a cofounder of Nijjor Manush, states:

> For a lot of people, there's this deep sense of loss and sadness around the fact that the city isn't just encroaching – the city is doing, in a way, through legislation and bureaucracy, what average people were doing to them in the streets in the 1970s. Corporations are just able to manage their racism, their sexism, their Islamophobia under the guise of legislation … It falls on all of us that want to be involved in raising that awareness with our communities to remind them of these struggles. We need to revive those histories.[41]

However, there was also some discomfort with this appropriation of 1970s struggles by the Save Brick Lane campaign, especially as some members of that generation believe that the redevelopment of the complex may well be the antidote for their dying businesses and therefore save their presence in the area. Some were supportive of the plans and hopeful that it might boost local trade. Restaurateur Shams Uddin, who arrived in Brick Lane at the beginning of the Bengali squatters' movement, said:

Save Brick Lane demonstration, June 2021 © Sarah Ainslie.

When customers finish their business with the shopping centre, they may come to my restaurant ... This is a good thing for our business.[42]

An older community activist who had been in Tower Hamlets since the 1980s expressed the same sentiment:

I know they keep saying 6000 people signed their petition – but you won't find any of the Bengali restaurants have signed that petition, and if you go and speak to them – I think they would welcome anything to bring back punters back to Brick Lane. It's not the development itself – but they want anything that will bring more people. But of course they wouldn't want an Indian restaurant in it because they want the traffic to come to them.

This generational division echoes that of the 1970s, when a constituent of older, middle-class businessmen and community leaders had counselled restraint, particularly when the vigilante groups emerged in response to NF violence and police failures. In part, those older men had been motivated by their perception of community interest and a belief in a system that they hoped would reward their moderation. It is also reminiscent of the struggles that Jacobs describes from the 1980s and 1990s in the contested development of Banglatown. In 2022 some of those who had been part of the more radical faction from the 1970s were now on the other side of the generational divide, counselling that there was something to be won by accepting some form of a proposal that might rescue the livelihood of the 'curry capital'.

Among those who were less supportive of the Save Brick Lane campaign, another grievance was that the coalition had partnered with The Spitalfields Trust, which has not historically been seen as a friend of the Bengali community. An older Bengali community activist who did not want to be named argued that though the campaign stated it was speaking on behalf of the Bengali community's interests, The Spitalfields Trust had been egregious in that relationship across the decades of regeneration since the 1970s, and could not claim to authentically hold those interests at heart:

> They are a white middle led organisation – because of *their* gentrification – they indirectly put-up prices of property, and all this gentrification that you hear about, if you want to blame someone – well blame them. So, it really doesn't make sense that they want to 'Save Brick Lane', when they are there in that campaign and the majority of Bengali owned businesses of Brick Lane are not...

He went on to state that:

> Historically, they have opposed anything to do with 'Bengaliness' or Bengali identity, at every stage they have opposed anything to do with Banglatown, they have always opposed anything Brick Lane Mosque tried to do ... anything. And they always use the thing about heritage – which is all fine – but at the same time they deny the existence of the Bengali community, so that talk about the Jewish community, the Huguenots – but never about the Bangladeshis who are currently there. So, there is that kind of contradiction –

and now they have jumped on this campaign with a few of our Bengali academics – none of whom are local and so that's why – they don't know that history.

This assessment of The Spitalfields Trust is reminiscent of Jane Jacobs' critique of how the organisation operated during previous regeneration projects in the 1980s and 1990s, cooperating with Bengali interests 'through a managed multiculturalism' and careful paternalism to ensure that their heritage interests were firmly prioritised. The community activist was not suggesting that the Spitalfields Trust was motivated by anything other than genuine heritage concerns. However, they suggested that even where they had built what seemed to be equal partnerships with Bengali activists, their frame of reference was felt to be one that restricted the role and position of the local Bengali community. The Trust's neat heritage aesthetic did not value the contributions of that community, unless it could be appropriated to serve what was seen to be their own narrow and racialised heritage interests. In the Spitalfields Trust's main 'Battle for Brick Lane' fundraising video, none of the speakers are from a Bengali background and the call for community-led participation only speaks of the site as a 'public asset'. They call for it to be used for 'public benefit' in general terms, with no reference at all to the local Bengali community, who only appear in muted black and white images from the 1970s and 1980s.

It was the composition of the Save Brick Lane coalition that was so problematic for many in the local area, who felt the campaign was based on an outsider's view of Brick Lane and had not engaged with the complex interests of the local community. The same community activist commented: 'I'm not doubting their sincerity – but they aren't rooted in Spitalfields, they don't know the pulse of the Spitalfields community'.

The younger activists were not unaware of these sentiments. Fatima acknowledged that there were local businesses and indeed residents who were attracted to the promise of improvement for the local community and were sceptical of the motivations of the coalition:

I remember one particular *Sasa* we spoke to on the estate on Spellman Street, I remember he said to us: 'Well, I've

bought my *bari* and I've had it for thirty years now, and I
don't have mortgage, so this doesn't affect me.' And we said,
'Well, you're right, it won't affect you, if you want to look at it
from that perspective. But it's not just about individuals, we're
talking about the collective, and the collective is what makes
a community, and you know people around here, you do your
shopping in Bangla Town, and in the Bangla Cash and Carry
on Hanbury Street, because you know these people – this is
what community is for.' I remember – when we talked to him
for a good about half an hour, and then he actually agreed to
sign the objection.

Fatima disagreed with the idea that the local community would
benefit, arguing that though these developments are often clothed
in warm rhetoric, they have a clear track record of alienating existing
communities and appealing to audiences that are considered more
lucrative and affluent:

> We're talking about literal exclusion of the local commu-
> nity. Whenever I walk down Brick Lane and I enter these
> new food businesses not a lot them serve halal meat, which is
> quite interesting because you're bang in the middle of Tower
> Hamlets where every other customer of yours is likely going
> to be a Muslim. For me, when businesses which can afford
> the rent of being located in Brick Lane come in but don't cater
> to the local community, that itself expands the gentrification
> and exclusion.

Frustrated with this misplaced hope for local benefit, she also
recalled that some of the opposition she encountered was less about
the proposal and more about her legitimacy as a woman to speak
on these issues – a view that, as a woman, she could not possibly
understand the complications of doing business on Brick Lane.
Nijjor Manush was, unlike the 1970s movement, a mixed-gender
group. It was made up mostly of second-generation Bengali young
people who utilised their education and social capital in deliberate
ways to further what they saw as protecting Bengali community
interests. In Fatima's accounts of their organising, the strong

female presence also meant that there was a different lens to what was valued; she often spoke of who was cooking and catering for their events, like the 'huge pots of *handesh*' (fried molasses and rice flour-based sweets) brought along by the mothers of other activists, which echoed conversations I had with women squatters like Husnara.

Interestingly, Fatima also spoke about the Truman Brewery proposal putting up property prices and the fact that Bengali families were not able to use the right-to-buy scheme to purchase their council properties as one key concern. This would seem to sit at odds with wider anti-gentrification campaigns that pinpoint the right-to-buy scheme as a key factor in the erosion of social housing stock. However, Fatima's concern about the impact on right-to-buy also shows a recognition that those anti-gentrification narratives can be insensitive to the economic realities for working-class Bengali communities, who have limited opportunity to acquire the security and wealth associated with home-ownership outside of the right-to-buy model.

On the other hand, studies on gentrification like the Runnymede Trust's 'Pushed to the Margins' report highlight that the depletion of social housing stock as a consequence of right-to-buy has directly disadvantaged Black and minority ethnic communities.[43] These communities are disproportionately lower income and have therefore traditionally relied more on social housing. They are now either housed in inadequate accommodation, struggle on the private rental market or wait on endless homeless lists in temporary accommodation. In sum, while right-to-buy may have given an asset boost to one generation, the next generation have paid a heavy price for it.

Despite these ongoing debates, Nijjor Manush's approach in the Save Brick Lane campaign has at its heart the idea that there are a broad range of communities in the area, all of whom are adversely affected by the Truman Brewery proposal. They connect those communities through a shared working-class identity. This is a shift away from the 1970s struggles of the Bengali squatter movement, for whom ethnicity was the single, critical node for community self-organisation. While *Race Today* campaigned around class, they were critical of uniting with the wider white

working class until there had been some self-organisation within
Black and Asian communities. Academics like Sarah Glynn, in
her book *Class, Ethnicity and Religion in the Bengali East End,*
lamented the failure of the Bengali community to situate themselves in the wider class-based discourse of the left in the 1970s.
The Save Brick Lane campaign led by Nijjor Manush appears to
demonstrate a shift in that discourse today. They offer a model
for how class, which has so often been manipulated to create
racialised divisions, can be mobilised to unite the interests of a
local, multi-ethnic community.

In September 2021 the local planning committee voted to
approve the Truman Brewery site proposal on the grounds that
they had no legal remit to object, despite the massive local opposition that had been galvanised. Kevin Brady, one of the councillors
on that committee, tweeted:

> The role of cllrs [councillors] on such committees is to deter-
> mine whether an app[lication] complies with policy. It was
> clear to me that this did and therefore there are no grounds
> for refusal. I appreciate there are a large number of people
> opposed but that is not itself a material planning considera-
> tion. It's important to recognise that committee don't create
> policy, they apply it. What I did suggest to officers is that they
> work with the lead member for planning to look at developing
> policy that address the very real concern that many commu-
> nities have about the impact of gentrification.

For many who oppose the complex, this typifies the nature of local
politics in a national framework that has allowed planning priorities to be dictated by finance, ignoring local communities. Fatima
pointed out, for example, the way that local councillors have offered
superficial tokens of care through the 'art-washing' of the area:

> I think there's this very paternalistic attitude towards commu-
> nity. Let's give them a new mural and let's indulge their
> nostalgia with *matir tan* mural [Bengali phrase meaning pull
> of the soil]. And then, let them do their little thing. But we'll
> just continue doing what we need to do.

'Mateer tan' mural painted by Mohammed Ali Aerosol,
Brick Lane © Seema Khalique.

She also highlighted the signage change at the opening of the
new Whitechapel Station in August 2021, which now features the
name of the station in Bengali script. She mocked the fact that
while local councillors proudly unveiled this token of their care for
the Bengali community, their cuts to funding for Bengali language
classes over the past few decades meant fewer of the younger generation would be able to read it.

Saif Osmani is also part of the Save Brick Lane coalition and a founder of the Bengali East End Heritage Society. His father, Osman Goni, was active in housing rights work in the late 1970s and was one of the founders of the Spitalfields Housing Cooperative. Saif describes himself as an artist and activist. He brought the Bengali East End Heritage Society into the Save Brick Lane coalition, keen to add to what he saw as Nijjor Manush's attention to historical struggles, and to connect the current campaign to anti-gentrification movements in other parts of London. For him, the coalition was attractive precisely because it brought together some of the older, heritage-focused organisations, which tended to be white and middle class, with younger Bangladeshi groups. In those conversations he argues that there is a developing understanding of how gentrification is impacting differently on diverse groups:

> … what I've witnessed within the last couple of years is there's a managed neglect, and I've used this term quite a lot, and other people have as well – or managed decline of existing social housing … and a lot of that, it ties into the Bangladeshi community and with ethnic minorities in Tower Hamlets. That's often the case of the Bangladeshis. Often women who are heads of families, or men who are sitting in quite post-war or pre-war sort of dark and rundown places, which might be of historic interest, but are forgotten. But what's actually happening is their social needs and requirements are becoming squeezed even further. So what you find is that sometimes where the area's expanding or changing, where there's a pocket park popping up and so forth, it tends to be for the affluent new incomers. But the existing community is not necessarily seeing the benefit. In fact, the embedded communities might and are seeing a new layer of displacement.

What Saif outlines here coincides with the experience described by Khosru when he complained of drug dealers congregating openly outside his estate, and the school pupils who described their estates as congested and noisy places to live. In contrast, the new build developments springing up around them were 'not for people like us'.

As a graduate of architecture, Saif argues that none of this is inevitable and that there is an insidiously racialised nature to how the local council has navigated investment and planning opportunities. Apart from pointing out that the early computer-generated images of the site's development did not include any south Asian or Bengali people, he argues that an increasingly hegemonic narrative about this displacement is that the Bengali community are willingly moving out of Tower Hamlets – that what is happening mirrors previous groups who have come to the East End, where the community organically moves on to other areas:

> In our experience when we went to get the views of people off of the estates locally and so forth, we found that that wasn't the case necessarily. It was that the Bangladeshi families had larger families. And so usually it was the youngest who had less options of staying and building up his own family or her own family. And they're in their 20s and 30s but their estate hadn't been done up, there were no improvements, they had less access to Brick Lane. So things hadn't improved overall for them.

The improvements promised by successive rounds of development and regeneration funding in the last few decades, now promised with the Truman Brewery proposal, have been unequally shared. He and others acknowledged that some people had moved away through choice. However, he also suggested that this framework of choice erases the decades of neglect and divestment that has led to the poor housing, lack of adequately sized properties and neighbourhoods of decline that have animated those choices.

Saif looks back to a time when Brick Lane was not just the shallow idea of a 'curry capital' but a wider cultural experience, with cafes that served the Bengali community, shops and music: 'It was a place that you would go to interact with people'. He describes the 'hipsterification' of Brick Lane and how, as a young man, he is able to navigate those changing cultural spaces, but 'my main identity group, my community' is not comfortable there anymore. That erosion of comfort may not take the form of the existential threat experienced by Bengali migrants in 1970s East London, where they were regular victims of random racialised attack, but nonetheless it speaks to what Adam Elliot-Cooper et al have described as the 'violence of un-homing'.[44] Fatima spoke about Brick Lane Jamme Masjid and pointed out, 'When you stand by the mosque, at the top there is a sign in Latin which says, "we are shadows". It means people come and go; they establish themselves, and through their own choice – not through coercion.'

Saif talked about grassroots community organising and the need for working closely with communities, to 'make them co-producers' in the planning process – to give local people autonomy to decide how their urban space is curated. He argues that communities have been disconnected from those conversations and have become reliant on the local council to deliver on their needs after winning increased representation there.

This idea of a gradual disconnection from community-based organising was something that Taj Ali, an independent scholar and activist from Luton, also spoke about. Like Fatima and Saif, Taj pointed to a sense that the earlier generation had secured considerable political power, at least at the local level, and that this had contributed to a decline in direct action politics in subsequent generations. For him this was problematic because of the continued prevalence of racism today:

> I think the first thing is when you look at the period of the seventies and eighties, the way racism existed is very different to how it exists today. I think now it's become more institutional – it's harder to call out. You can literally get away with – without saying a racial slur, you're discriminating in housing, you're discriminating against them in so many different fields. When we look at the statistics, I think I was reading 24 per cent of Bangladeshis live in overcrowded housing. We're talking about the squatters' movement in the 1970s, but people are being priced out of their areas now. This is almost invisible violence and it's the hardest to call out.

He went on to talk about his experiences at Warwick University and how there were many south Asian heritage students in the university, but very few of them came from socio-economic backgrounds like his. Taj linked this to the 'post-racial society' narrative, which traded on the 'myth of meritocracy' that 'if you just work hard, you can escape your poverty':

And on the face of it, when we talk about BAME statistics, it looks like we've achieved diversity in universities. You look at the Tory leadership election and everyone's talking about how we've ended racism because we've got Asian people deporting the rest of us now. So I think this kind of surface-level representation – it appeals to this kind of feel-good narrative. And it's very superficial. For me, I think the way to kind of combat that is to link race and class, to talk about the fact that people growing up in poverty are disproportionately ethnic minorities.

Taj argues that this kind of 'invisible violence' in one sense makes the kind of mobilisations that were possible in the 1970s and 1980s more difficult to organise. He argues that we have become a more 'atomised society' where the 'neoliberal myth' has prevailed. He also argues that the possibility for mobilising anti-racist movements is also limited now because there is much more division between minoritised ethnic communities:

When I speak to some of the people involved with the Asian youth movements, they talk about how Hindus, Sikhs, Muslims – they would organise together. The Black and South Asian communities were organised together because they were experiencing the same problems. And now ... these communities have become divided.

One of the conclusions Taj draws is that state funding has become part of the problem. Like Nurul Hoque's East End Community School's petition to secure funding and premises from the local council in the 1970s, securing funds catalysed what Fatima called the 'co-opting' of south Asian struggles into the state system, effectively neutralising their more radical demands. For Taj, this also inhibited opportunities to build solidarity across different movements:

I've seen with austerity and cuts to public services – David Cameron championed this idea of the Big Society, we distributed funds to communities, and I think now what's happened is communities are competing against one another for funding. So we've become increasingly atomised in that sense. It's meant that people are holding their tongue a bit more. Anti-racist movements that were very grassroots have become institutionalised in the boardrooms. Nowadays the issue of diversity and inclusion is a PR exercise. Companies make a lot of money from it.

Taj argued that the key to organising against the latest iteration of 'invisible violence' is to return to and innovate from some of the key tenets of community organising that were so powerful in the 1970s. It is time to return to grassroots organising, to rekindle small conversations and grow power from the bottom up. This is not to reject or dismiss the need to engage with and win representation at the local and national political level, but it was to remember that this alone was never enough:

I'm not against representation. I'm not against having good people in positions of power. But I think it's important to remember the grassroots and too many times I've seen people forget the grassroots and get into these positions and hold their tongue on issues affecting us. And just to contrast with what representation was like in the 1960s, if we look at the Indian Workers Association – a massive organisation, they had numerous different groups, but in Southall at one point I think they said half the adult males in certain parts of Southall were members of the Indian Workers Association. And what they would do ... they were saying that the Labour Party and the Conservative Party would take the Indian Workers Association very seriously because whilst they might not be a political party, they could influence the votes of thousands of south Asians. So they would grill political candidates on their views on immigration, on their views on discrimination, and how to tackle racism. And if those Indian Workers Association members felt that these candidates were not supporting them, they wouldn't support them in any election. And there were cases where they refused to support candidates. And when we look at the industrial disputes, when the Indian Workers Association got involved in industrial disputes, the employees were taken very seriously because they knew that they could mobilise thousands of South Asians from other industries as well. And that was the power of the grassroots. That was the power of organising outside of a party structure, but still influencing policy. So I think we need to move away from this idea that the only way to make change is through a political party – I think there's plenty of ways that you can make a difference. Ideally, I think we do need good people in political parties, of course, but we can't forget the other avenues in which we can make change. When we look at how we defeated the EDL in Luton, it was through grassroots mobilisations. It wasn't through a bill in the Houses of Parliament.

Taj is not from the local Bengali community, but in some ways his sentiments align with those of Julie Begum, a dedicated local community activist. Julie was born and brought up in the Tower Hamlets area and finds the debates around the Truman Brewery over-inflated and distracting. For Julie, the Bengali community in Tower Hamlets has life and vibrancy well beyond the strip of Brick Lane that has caught so much political attention. Her work sees her speaking to and organising with young and old people in communities all over the borough. She argued that on the ground people were working in multi-cultural and working-class communities, finding ways to piece together community in difficult times. She found the tensions around the Save Brick Lane campaign on both sides a distraction that did not speak to the everyday concerns of the wider community. The 'creativity and cultural life of the Bengali community isn't just in Brick Lane' and even if the Truman Brewery complex goes ahead, 'it won't be the death of the community there – it will be just another one of those changes that happens', she said.

The debates around the Truman Brewery proposal highlight the challenges of agreeing what a community's interests are. Wherever one sits, the debate itself has begun a valuable conversation around what is happening to Brick Lane, a multi-generational conversation which recognises that business and residential interests are not necessarily aligned, and that narratives about solidarity within and across communities need to be strengthened by honest reflection and evaluation.

After planning approval was granted in September 2021, the Save Brick Lane campaign raised enough funds to launch a judicial review of the decision. However, before this judicial review was heard there was a dramatic shift in the local political landscape when councillor Kevin Brady and Mayor John Biggs – who had effectively granted the proposal – were dramatically ousted at the local elections in May 2022. The new Mayor, Lutfur Rahman, who has a long and fractious history with the local Labour Party, stood as a candidate for a new, left-of-Labour party called Aspire. He has promised to review the planning permission granted to the Truman Brewery proposal, though the legalities are unclear. Whether he has the power to independently reverse the decision remains under discussion.

Nearly fifty years after the events of the Bengali Squatters' movement, we find ourselves in a decade that bristles with tensions similar to those that saw out the 1970s: economic turbulence, crippling inflation, a winter of discontent and politicians that seem incapable of grasping the desperate needs of those who are most buffeted by these forces. The fight over the Truman Brewery Complex now carries the added burdens of what has become known as the 'cost-of-living' crisis, a catchphrase used to describe the perilous economic situation that so many communities face in Britain today. With inflation at record-levels, low-income families are experiencing potentially fatal forms of poverty at depths and rates that were familiar to the Victorian tenements in and around Brick Lane in the 1870s and Bengalis squatters in the 1970 – but were thought to have been eliminated in twenty-first-century Britain.

During the pandemic, we were reassured that we were 'all in this together'. We were urged to perform our civic duty: to look after each other and our communities by complying with the public health measures that were imposed – even as we later learned that the inner circle of government partied behind closed doors. The idea of a shared burden was far from the truth. In reality, Bengali people in Tower Hamlets died at twice the rate of their white peers in the same borough. One reason was that Bengali people work in the most public facing sectors, including retail, hospitality and transport, which meant that they had greater exposure to the virus. They are also most likely to be involved in key-worker roles in health and education services – particularly at the lowest tier of those workforces – and so are again less likely to have the flexibility and shielding afforded to their managers, and are more likely to face greater exposure in their work. In addition to their employment profile, the Bengali community in Tower Hamlets continues to face housing hardship and is likely to live in smaller, overcrowded conditions, without access to outdoor space. All these factors made conditions ripe for the virus to spread.

But the excess of deaths from Covid-19 was not an aberration from an otherwise rosy picture of equality. Just like other Black and minority ethnic working-class communities, the Bengali community have faced decades of low-paid and insecure work and continue (alongside Pakistani people) to have the lowest average hourly wage. The statistics around income for Bengali young people in Tower Hamlets remain stubbornly low, and despite significant gains in their educational outcomes they have not seen similar returns in their employment outcomes. This in turn means that they will have lower resilience to the cost-of-living crisis and are overrepresented in poverty measures. Tower Hamlets has the highest rate of poverty and child poverty in London. More broadly, Bengali people are 4.2 times more likely to be in 'relative poverty' (60 per cent below median income) compared to their white counterparts, and three times more likely to experience 'deep poverty'.[45] Those families are suffering food insecurity, material deprivation and fuel poverty at a level that brings them close to destitution. Their ability to endure the cost-of-living crisis will not be brought about by swapping to cheaper supermarket brands, as one Tory MP suggested.[46]

Austerity cuts by the Conservative government over the last decade have also had a disproportionate impact on Black and minoritised ethnic groups and have whittled away their capacity to build financial resilience. Regressive tax benefit measures like the universal credit cap, the under-occupancy penalty and the two-child limit on child benefit have taken away more money from these communities than their white peers (£806 compared to £454).[47] This is largely down to the disproportionate number of Black and minoritised ethnic communities in low-paid work and therefore their greater reliance on benefits to top up their low income, rather than the much-peddled myth that social security claimants are feckless and workshy. In fact, a recent study highlighted that austerity measures have not just exacted punishment on purses, but that over 300,000 excess deaths can be linked directly to the austerity measures that the government has imposed since 2010.[48]

It was during the early part of the Covid-19 pandemic that George Floyd, a forty-six-year-old Black man, was murdered by a white police officer in the US city of Minneapolis as he cried out 'I can't breathe'. The Black Lives Matter movement rippled around the world and the phrase became symbolic of the anger against institutionalised racism that continues to live on so actively in the police force, not just in America but around the world. The BLM protests in the US inspired a wave of protests around the UK, one of which famously saw the statue of Edward Colston, Bristolian trader of enslaved Africans, torn down and thrown into the harbour. In many ways, George Floyd's murder and the BLM movement triggered a moment of reflection. The timing – just as the UK was facing a death toll that registered just how disproportionately Black and Asian people were dying from Covid-19 because of the socio-economic position described above – meant that even those usually indifferent to claims of racism had to pause and assess the inequities that were revealed.

But the complexities of these inequalities are too often overshadowed by a corrosive mainstream politics that has, in recent years, focused on 'taking back control'. The 'hostile environment' policy has resulted in the Windrush scandal, where Caribbean migrants – British citizens – were deprived of public services, rights to housing, employment and even healthcare because they were unable to 'prove' their citizenship status. Meanwhile, Shamima Begum, a young Bengali girl from Bethnal Green who was groomed to join ISIS in Syria in 2015, has been deprived of citizenship and rendered stateless. We have witnessed the ongoing 'culture wars', which have labelled everything from footballers taking the knee to the calls to decolonise our school curriculum as un-patriotic. But then, ironically, we also have our first minority ethnic Prime Minister, Rishi Sunak. A child of immigrant Indians and a practicing Hindu, he sits in a more diverse cabinet than the UK has ever known.

That few who are serious about anti-racist politics are celebrating Sunak is telling. He is a billionaire, private-school educated Oxford graduate who has supported the Conservative government in all their regressive measures over the past seven years. He was elected by 190 Conservative MPs. In his short political career he has supported the Police, Crime and Courts Sentencing Act (2022) and the Public Order Bill (2022), which have come about in response to the kind of direct-action tactics which saw the Colston statue ripped down, and tactics employed more widely by groups like Extinction Rebellion, Just Stop Oil and Insulate Britain. He has supported the Rwanda deportation policy that seeks to deport asylum seekers who land in Britain to secure facilities in Rwanda. As Chancellor, he supported and pursued austerity measures despite their disproportionate impact on Black and minority ethnic communities and has hinted that he will continue to do so as prime minister.

There is little merit in representation if diversity simply means more of the same harmful policies that are indifferent to or actively harm Black and Asian communities. If anything, that diversity gives a dangerous form of immunity to anti-racist challenge. It also overlooks the class-based dimension of representation – the Bengali community in 1970s London may not have been able to find solidarity with the white working-class community it faced so much violence from, but they are just as unlikely in 2022 to feel aligned with a billionaire Asian prime minister. This account of the 1970s Bengali squatters' movement is not a glimpse into a remote past – the challenges of the hostile environment policy, the potential for austerity 2.0, and the complexities of the intersections between race and class are as pronounced now as they were nearly half a century ago.

This book began life in the snatches of stories my parents told me as they struggled to build a life for themselves in a country which they had not imagined would become their lifelong home. Their early misgivings about settling here were shaped by their experiences of housing discrimination and racism, but despite those challenges they, like the Bengali community in London and in the UK more widely, have made their home here. This book has the stories of Bengali migrants who arrived in the 1960s and 1970s at its heart. It seeks to share their stories because, up until now, the popular and academic research on this period have ignored or diminished these events and their contributions to the wider anti-racist struggles of this period. Bengali squatters, whether they considered themselves activists or simply home-makers, were connected to a much longer history of empire, colonialism and migration. The competing ideas around belonging that were at the heart of their squatter struggles cannot be understood outside of those complex historical geographies.

This book has tried to offer space to people who have never been invited to tell their stories before to trace how their battles to claim and make home were both culturally connected to Sylhet and the community they were fighting to build in Spitalfields. Those experiences deserve their place in our understanding of 1970s social history of the East End, but they could also offer inspiration for the struggles that lie ahead, helping us to challenge the class and race-based attacks on our communities. bell hooks said we must struggle to remember not for the sake of nostalgia but because the act of remembering 'serves to illuminate and transform the present.'[49] Recovering my parents' and this community's history is, I hope, one small contribution to thinking about our past, and an encouragement to others to conduct the anti-racist work of recovering our hidden histories in the future.

NOTES

1 Office for National Statistics, 'Population and household estimates, England and Wales: Census 2021', www.ons.gov.uk, 2021.
2 Trust for London, 'London's Poverty Profile 2020', www.trustfor-london.org.uk, 2020.
3 Tower Hamlets Council, *Housing Evidence Base*, 2016, p3.
4 Ibid, p12.
5 Christian Weaver, 'Awaab Ishak's death shed light on a social housing scandal. Now we have a brief chance to fix it', www.theguardian.com, 23 November 2022.

6   Tower Hamlets Council, 'Understanding the impact of Covid-19 in Tower Hamlets', 2020, p2.

7   James Nazroo and Laia Bécares, 'Ethnic Inequalities in COVID-19 Mortality: A Consequence of Persistent Racism', Runnymede Trust, 2021, pp3-4.

8   Ibid.

9   Office for National Statistics, 'Updating ethnic contrasts in deaths involving the coronavirus (COVID-19), England: 24 January 2020 to 31 March 2021', www.ons.gov.uk, 2021.

10 Adam Elliott-Cooper, Phil Hubbard, Loretta Lees, 'Moving beyond Marcuse: Gentrification, displacement and the violence of un-homing', *Progress in Human Geography*, Vol. 44, 2020, pp492-509.

11 Jane Jacobs, *Edge of Empire: Postcolonialism and the City*, Routledge: London, UK, 1996.

12 The Spitalfields Trust, 'The Spitalfields Trust: A Brief History', www.thespitalfieldstrust.com. Accessed 7 February 2023.

13 Jacobs, op cit, pp77.

14 Ibid, pp75-80.

15 Spitalfields Trust, op cit.

16 Charlie Forman, *Spitalfields: A Battle for Land*, Hilary Shipman: London, 1989, p135.

17 Spitalfields Trust, op cit.

18 Jacobs, op cit, p83.

19 Forman, op cit, p141.

20 Jacobs, op cit, p87.

21 Ibid, pp86-7.

22 Ibid, p99.

23 Claire Alexander, 'Contested memories: The Shahid Minar and the struggle for diasporic space', *Ethnic & Racial Studies*, Vol. 36(4), 2013, pp590-610.

24 Ibid, p592.

25 Ibid, p591.

26 Jacobs, op cit, p97.

27 Ibid, p102.

28 Claire Alexander, Seán Carey, Suzanne Hall, Julia King, and Sundeep Lidher, 'Beyond Banglatown: Continuity, Change and New Urban Economies in Brick Lane', University of Manchester, 2020.

29 Sean Carey, 'The rise and fall of Brick Lane's 'Curry Capital'', *Anthropology Today*, Vol. 37, No. 5, 2021, p3.

30 Alexander et al 2020, op cit, p16.

31 Ibid.

32 Carey, op cit, p6.

33 Phil Hubbard, 'Hipsters on our high streets: Consuming the gentrification frontier', *Sociological Research Online*, 21(3), 2016, p107.
34 Ibid, p108.
35 Adam Elliott Cooper, Phil Hubbard, and Loretta Lees, 'Sold out? The right-to-buy, gentrification and working-class displacements in London', *The Sociological Review*, Vol. 68, No. 6, 2020, p1358.
36 Claire Alexander, Seán Carey, Suzanne Hall, and Julia King, 'Revisiting Brick Lane: The Impact of COVID-19 on an Ethnically Diverse High Street', The Runnymede Trust, 2021, p1.
37 Anne Kershen, *Strangers, Aliens and Asians: Huguenots, Jews and Bangladeshis in Spitalfields 1666-2000*, Routledge: London, 2004.
38 Alexander et al 2020, op cit, p4.
39 https://nijjormanush.com.
40 https://nijjormanush.com/save-brick-lane-campaign.
41 Sotez Choudhury quoted in Taj Ali, 'The Battle for Brick Lane', www.tribunemag.co.uk/2021/04/the-battle-for-brick-lane, 23 April 2021.
42 Aina J. Khan, 'Towers Rise Over London's Brick Lane, Clouding Its Future', www.nytimes.com, 5 January 2022.
43 Adam Almeida, 'Pushed to the Margins', The Runnymede Trust, 2021.
44 Elliott-Cooper at al 2020, op cit, pp492-509.
45 Daniel Edmiston, Shabna Begum, Mandeer Kataria, 'Falling Faster Amidst a Cost-of-Living Crisis', The Runnymede Trust, October 2021.
46 Shropshire Star, 'Minister labelled "out of touch" for suggesting shoppers swap to value brands', https://www.shropshirestar.com, 4 May 2022.
47 Sarah Hall, Kimberly Mcintosh, Eva Neitzert, Laura Pottinger, Kalwinder Sandhu, Mary-Ann Stephenson, Howard Reed, and Leonie Taylor, 'Intersecting Inequalities: The Impact of Austerity on Black and Minority Ethnic Women in the UK', Runnymede Trust, Women's Budget Group, 2017.
48 Patrick Butler, 'Over 330,000 excess deaths in Great Britain linked to austerity, finds study', www.guardian.com, 5 October 2022.
49 bell hooks, 'Yearning: Race, gender, and cultural politics', *Hypatia*, 7(2), 1992, p147.

Acknowledgements

This book may have one named author, but it was written through the efforts of an unknowable number of people, whose experiences, stretching across time and space, form the heart of this book.

This work would never have materialised without the generosity and goodwill of my research participants. I am indebted to all of them for the extraordinary stories they shared and the time they gave me. Thanks also to all the archivists who helped me gather materials, in particular the staff (many of whom I now claim as my friends) at Tower Hamlets Local History Library and Archives, the George Padmore Institute, Leila Hassan and Darcus Howe Legacy and the British Film Archives. I am also grateful to Professor Kavita Datta, Professor Alastair Owens and Dr Olivia Sheringham for their supervision and support during my PhD studies at QMUL and all my fellow doctoral students, who were always so kind and interested in my work. Many of the portrait photographs featured are the work of Seema Khalique, who gave her time and attention so generously. I also must thank everyone at Lawrence Wishart, especially Jumanah Younis, whose careful editing and advice have been critical to this work.

I have been so incredibly fortunate to have had so many good people in my life and to have met so many more during this process; people who have offered unswerving support and encouragement from when I first came up with the idea, to the bleak days when the slog seemed endless. Old and new friends who nudged me to carry on when I was tired, who offered advice and counsel when I confronted challenges, gave me time and space to write when I felt crowded. There are too many of you to name here, but every one of you helped me see this project through and for that I am grateful. I owe a special debt to Julie Mukherjee for her friendship, encourage-ment and for always keeping my politics in check.

I started this book as a teacher and finished this book as head of research at the Runnymede Trust; in both those workplaces I have been blessed with relationships of care, affection and intellectual challenge, and these have helped shape this book and my journey with it. I need to thank Halima Begum in particular, for her unre-lenting support, and for opening so many doors and opportunities for me – I have learnt so much from you.

I must of course thank my parents, Abdul Masabbir and Guljahan Begum, who never had an opportunity to pursue an education for themselves – but whose story inspired this research and book. This is their achievement, just as much as it is mine. To all my sisters and brothers, Rasna, Shamle, Abdul Hafez, Zinath, Ayesha and Abdul Salam, and my niece Suraiya; you are and always will be my greatest advocates – I would never have started or lasted this journey without your love and encouragement.

And finally, thanks to my daughter, Anisah, and my son, Ihsan. You are the greatest gifts of my life and I hope when you are both older, you will appreciate the journey we took together.

Alhamdulillah.

Index